Workshop on Graph-based Methods for Natural Language Processing 2011

(TextGraphs-6)

Held at ACL HLT 2011

Portland, Oregon, USA
23 June 2011

ISBN: 978-1-61839-243-5

Printed from e-media with permission by:

Curran Associates, Inc.
57 Morehouse Lane
Red Hook, NY 12571

Some format issues inherent in the e-media version may also appear in this print version.

Printed by Curran Associates, Inc. (2011)

For permission requests, please contact the Association for Computational Linguistics at the address below.

Association for Computational Linguistics
209 N. Eighth Street
Stroudsburg, Pennsylvania 18360

Phone: 1-570-476-8006
Fax: 1-570-476-0860

acl@aclweb.org

Additional copies of this publication are available from:

Curran Associates, Inc.
57 Morehouse Lane
Red Hook, NY 12571 USA
Phone: 845-758-0400
Fax: 845-758-2634
Email: curran@proceedings.com
Web: www.proceedings.com

Preface

TextGraphs is at its SIXTH edition! This confirms that two seemingly distinct disciplines, graph theoretic models and computational linguistics, are in fact intimately connected, with a large variety of Natural Language Processing (NLP) applications adopting efficient and elegant solutions from graph-theoretical framework.

The TextGraphs workshop series addresses a broad spectrum of research areas and brings together specialists working on graph-based models and algorithms for natural language processing and computational linguistics, as well as on the theoretical foundations of related graph-based methods.

This workshop series is aimed at fostering an exchange of ideas by facilitating a discussion about both the techniques and the theoretical justification of the empirical results among the NLP community members. Spawning a deeper understanding of the basic theoretical principles involved, such interaction is vital to the further progress of graph-based NLP applications.

The submissions to this year workshop were high quality and also the selection process was more competitive than in previous editions. We selected 9 out of 16 papers for an acceptance rate of about 55%. The predominant topics of such contributions are, as usual, semantic similarity and word sense disambiguation. However, thanks also to the special theme of this year in the area of machine learning, i.e. *Graphs in Structured Input/Output Learning*, a larger use of principled statistical approaches can be observed. This trend will be nicely supported by the very interesting invited talk by Prof. Hal Daumé III on advanced and practical machine learning, entitled: *Structured Prediction need not be Slow*.

Finally, we are grateful to the European Community project, EternalS: "Trustworthy Eternal Systems via Evolving Software, Data and Knowledge" (project number FP7 247758) for continuing to sponsor our workshop.

The organizers
Irina Matveeva, Lluís Màrquez, Alessandro Moschitti and Fabio Massimo Zanzotto
Portland, June 2011

Structured Prediction need not be Slow

Invited talk

Hal Daumé III
University of Maryland – College Park
hal@umiacs.umd.edu

Abstract

Classic algorithms for predicting structured data (eg., graphs, trees, etc.) rely on expensive (sometimes intractable) inference at test time. In this talk, I'll discuss several recent approaches that enable computationally efficient (eg., linear-time) prediction at test time. These approaches fall in the category of learning algorithms that optimize accuracy for some fixed notion of efficiency. I'll conclude by considering the question: can a learning algorithm figure out how to make fast predictions on its own?

Organizers:

Irina Matveeva, Dieselpoint Inc., USA
Alessandro Moschitti, University of Trento, Italy
Lluís Màrquez, Technical University of Catalonia, Spain
Fabio Massimo Zanzotto, University of Rome "Tor Vergata", Italy

Program Committee:

Eneko Agirre, University of the Basque Country, Spain
Roberto Basili, University of Rome "Tor Vergata", Italy
Ulf Brefeld, Yahoo! Barcelona, Spain
Razvan Bunescu, Ohio University, USA
Nicola Cancedda, Xerox Research Centre Europe, France
William Cohen, Carnegie Mellon University, USA
Andras Csomai, Google USA
Mona Diab, Columbia University, USA
Gael Dias, Universidade da Beira Interior, Portugal
Michael Gamon, Microsoft Research, Redmond, USA
Thomas Gaertner, University of Bonn and Fraunhofer IAIS, Germany
Andrew Goldberg, University of Wisconsin, USA
Richard Johansson, Trento University, Italy
Lillian Lee, Cornell University, USA
Ryan McDonald, Google Research, USA
Rada Mihalcea, University of North Texas, USA
Animesh Mukherjee, CSL Lab, ISI Foundation, Torino, Italy
Bo Pang, Yahoo! Research, USA
Patrick Pantel, USC Information Sciences Institute, USA
Daniele Pighin, Technical University of Catalonia, Spain
Uwe Quasthoff, University of Leipzig, Germany
Dragomir Radev, University of Michigan, USA
Dan Roth, University of Illinois at Urbana Champaign, USA
Aitor Soroa, University of the Basque Country, Spain
Veselin Stoyanov, Johns Hopkins University, USA
Swapna Somasundaran, Siemens Corporate Research, USA

Invited Speaker:

Hal Daumé III, University of Maryland, USA

Official Sponsor:

ETERNALS: European Coordinate Action on Trustworthy Eternal Systems via Evolving Software, Data and Knowledge (project number FP7 247758)

Table of Contents

TextGraphs-6 Program

Thursday, June 23, 2011

9:00–9:15 Opening Remarks

Special Track Session: "Graphs in Structured Input/Output Learning"

10:30–11:00 Coffee Break

Session 1

11:25–12:30 Invited talk by Hal Daumé III: *Structured Prediction need not be Slow*

12:30–14:00 Lunch Break

Thursday, June 23, 2011 (continued)

Session 2

14:00–14:25 *Using a Wikipedia-based Semantic Relatedness Measure for Document Clustering*
Majid Yazdani and Andrei Popescu-Belis

14:25–14:50 *GrawlTCQ: Terminology and Corpora Building by Ranking Simultaneously Terms, Queries and Documents using Graph Random Walks*
Clément de Groc, Xavier Tannier and Javier Couto

14:50–15:15 *Simultaneous Similarity Learning and Feature-Weight Learning for Document Clustering*
Pradeep Muthukrishnan, Dragomir Radev and Qiaozhu Mei

15:15–15:45 Coffee Break

Session 3

15:45–16:10 *Unrestricted Quantifier Scope Disambiguation*
Mehdi Manshadi and James Allen

16:10–16:35 *From ranked words to dependency trees: two-stage unsupervised non-projective dependency parsing*
Anders Søgaard

16:35–17:30 Panel Discussion

17:30–17:45 Closing Session

A Combination of Topic Models with Max-margin Learning for Relation Detection

Dingcheng Li
University of Minnesota
Twin Cities, MN 55455
lixxx345@umn.edu

Swapna Somasundaran
Siemens Corporate Research
Princeton, NJ 08540
swapna.somasundaran@siemens.com

Amit Chakraborty
Siemens Corporate Research
Princeton, NJ 08540
amit.chakraborty@siemens.com

Abstract

This paper proposes a novel application of a supervised topic model to do entity relation detection (ERD). We adapt Maximum Entropy Discriminant Latent Dirichlet Allocation (MEDLDA) with mixed membership for relation detection. The ERD task is reformulated to fit into the topic modeling framework. Our approach combines the benefits of both, maximum-likelihood estimation (MLE) and max-margin estimation (MME), and the mixed membership formulation enables the system to incorporate heterogeneous features. We incorporate different features into the system and perform experiments on the ACE 2005 corpus. Our approach achieves better overall performance for precision, recall and Fmeasure metrics as compared to SVM-based and LLDA-based models.

1 Introduction

Entity relation detection (ERD) aims at finding relations between pairs of Named Entities (NEs) in text. Availability of annotated corpora (NIST, 2003; Doddington et al., 2004) and introduction of shared tasks (e.g. (Farkas et al., 2010; Carreras and Màrquez, 2005)) has spurred a large amount of research in this field in recent times. Researchers have used supervised and semi-supervised approaches (Hasegawa et al., 2004; Mintz et al., 2009; Jiang, 2009), and explored rich features (Kambhatla, 2004), kernel design (Culotta and Sorensen, 2004; Zhou et al., 2005; Bunescu and Mooney, 2005; Qian et al., 2008) and inference algorithms (Chan and Roth, 2011), to detect predefined relations between NEs.

In this work, we explore if and how the latent semantics of the text can help in detecting entity relations. For this, we adapt the Latent Dirichlet Allocation (LDA) approach to solve the ERD task. Specifically, we present a ERD system based on Maximum Entropy Discriminant Latent Dirichlet Allocation (MEDLDA). MEDLDA (Zhu et al., 2009), is an extension of Latent Dirichlet Allocation (LDA) that combines capability of capturing latent semantics with the discriminative capabilities of SVM.

There are a number of challenges in employing the LDA framework for ERD. Latent Dirichlet Allocation and its supervised extensions such as Labeled LDA (LLDA) (Ramage et al., 2009) and supervised LDA (sLDA) (Blei and McAuliffe, 2008) are powerful generative models that capture the underlying semantics of texts. However, they have trouble discovering marginal classes and easily employing rich feature sets, both of which are important for ERD. We overcome the first drawback by employing a MEDLDA framework, which integrates maximum likelihood estimation (MLE) and maximum margin estimation (MME). Specifically, it is a combination of sLDA and support vector machines (SVMs). Further, in order to employ rich and heterogeneous features we introduce a separate exponential family distribution for each feature, similar to (Shan et al., 2009), into our MEDLDA model.

We formulate the relation detection task within the topic model framework as follows. Pairs of NE mentions[1] and the text between them is considered

[1] Adopting the terminology used in the Automatic Context Extraction (ACE) program (NIST, 2003), specific NE instances are called mentions.

as *mini-document*. Each mini-document has a relation type (analogous to the response variable in the supervised topic model). The topic model infers the topic (relation type) distribution of the mini-documents. The supervised topic model discovers a latent topic representation of the mini-documents and a response parameter distribution. The topic representation is discovered with observed response variables during training. During testing, the topic distribution of each mini-document can form a prediction of the relation types.

We carry out experiments to measure the effectiveness of our approach and compare it to SVM-based and LLDA-based models, as well as to a previous work using the same corpora. We also measure and analyze the effectiveness of incorporating different features in our model relative to other models. Our approach exhibits better overall precision, recall and Fmeasure than baseline systems. We also find that the MEDLDA-based approach shows consistent capability for incorporation and improvement due to a variety of heterogeneous features.

The rest of the paper is organized as follows. We describe the proposed model in Section 2 and the features that we explore in this work in Section 3. Section 4 describes the data, experiments, results and analyses. We discuss the related work in Section 5 before concluding in Section 6.

2 MEDLDA for Relation Detection

MEDLDA is an extension of LDA proposed by Zhu, Ahmed and Xing (2009). LDA is itself unsupervised and the results are often hard to interpret. However, with the addition of supervised information (such as response variables), the resulting topic models have much better predictive power for classification and regression. In our work, we use relation annotations from the ACE (ACE, 2000 2005) corpus to provide the supervision. NE pairs within a sentence, and the text between them are considered as a mini-document. Each mini-document is assumed to be composed of a set of topics. The topic model trained with these mini-documents given their relation type label can generate topics biased toward relation types. Thus, the trained topic model will have good predictive power on relation types.

We first describe the MEDLDA model from (Zhu et al., 2009) and then describe how we adapt it for relation detection using mixed membership extensions.

2.1 MEDLDA

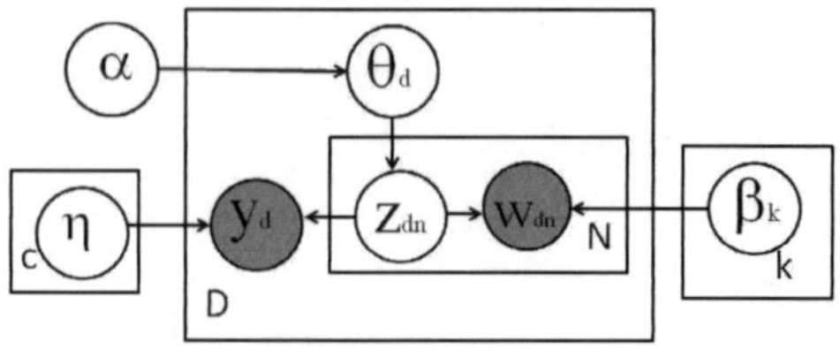

Figure 1: MEDLDA

The MEDLDA model described in (Zhu et al., 2009) is illustrated in Figure 1[2].

Here, α is a k-dimensional parameter of a Dirichlet distribution, $\beta_{1:k}$ are the parameters for k component distribution over the words. Each component refers to a topic. In a collection of documents D, each document $w_{1:N}$ is generated from a sequence of topics $z_{1:N}$. θ is a k-dimensional topic distribution variable, which is sampled from a Dirichlet distribution $Dir(\alpha)$. Like common LDAs, MEDLDA uses independence assumption for a finite set of random variables $z_1, ..., z_n$ which are independent and identically distributed, conditioned on the parameter θ. Like sLDA, MEDLDA is a supervised model. A response variable Y connected to each document is added for incorporating supervised side information. The supervised side information is expected to make MEDLDA topic discoveries more interpretable. Zhu, Ahmed and Xing's (2009) MEDLDA model can be used in both regression and classification. Concretely, Y is drawn from $\eta_{1:c}$, a c k-dimensional vector which can be derived from suitable statistical model. In our work, c is the number of relation types. Note that the plate diagram for MEDLDA is quite similar to sLDA (Blei and McAuliffe, 2008). But there is a difference – sLDA focuses on building regression models, and thus the response variable Y in sLDA is generated by a normal distribution.

Based on the plate diagram, the joint distribution of latent and observable variables for our MEDLDA-

[2](Zhu et al., 2009) do not have this plate digram in their paper; rather, we create this illustration from the description of their model.

based relation detection is given by

$$p(\theta, \mathbf{z}, \mathbf{w}, \mathbf{y}|\alpha, \beta_{1:k}, \eta_{1:c})$$
$$= \prod_{d=1}^{D} p(\theta_d|\alpha) \times \Big(\prod_{n=1}^{N} p(z_{dn}|\theta_d) p(w_{dn}|z_{dn}, \beta_{1:k}) \Big)$$
$$\times\, p(y_d|z_{d1:dN}, \eta_{1:c}) \quad (1)$$

Another important difference from sLDA lies in the fact that MEDLDA does joint learning with both MME and MLE. The joint learning is done in two stages, unsupervised topic discovery and multi-class classification (we refer the reader to (Zhu et al., 2009) for details). During training, EM algorithms are utilized to infer the posterior distribution of the hidden variables θ, $\mathbf{z}$ and η. In testing, the trained models are used to predict relation types y.

2.2 Mixed Membership MEDLDA

Although the MEDLDA model described above can be applied to the relation detection and classification task, a few modifications are necessary before it can be effective in predicting relation types. Mainly, a limitation of LDA or other existing topic models is the difficulty in incorporating rich features. This is because LDA is designed to handle data points with homogeneous features such as words. But for relation detection, like many other NLP tasks, it is important to have the flexibility of incorporating part-of-speech tags, named entities, grammatical dependencies and other linguistic features. We overcome this limitation by introducing a separate exponential family distribution for each feature similar to (Shan et al., 2009). Thus, our MEDLDA-based relation detection model is really a mixed-member Bayesian network. Figure 2 illustrates our model with this extension.

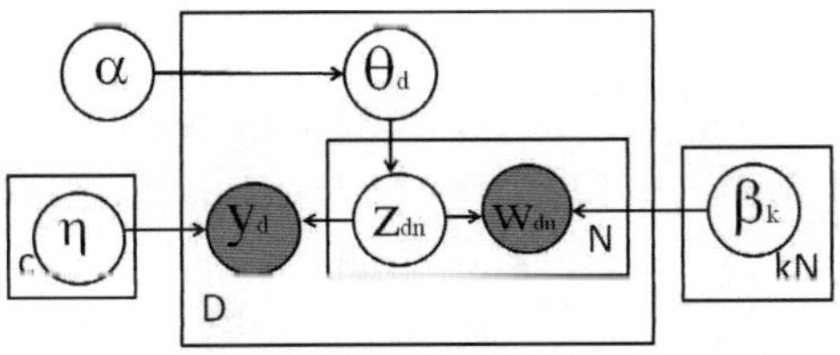

Figure 2: Mixed Membership MEDLDA

Figure 2 is very similar to Figure 1; the only difference is that the topic component number k is now kN. The generative process for each document this model is as follows:

1. Sample a component proportion $\theta_d \sim$ **Dirichlet**(α),

2. For each feature like word, part-of-speech, named entity in the document,

   (a) For $n \in \{1, ..., \text{N}\}$, sample $z_{dn} = i \sim$ **Discrete**(θ_d)

   (b) For $n \in \{1,...,\text{N}\}$, sample $w_{dn} \sim P(w_{dn}|\beta^d_{ni})$

3. Sample the relation type label from a softmax($\bar{z}$,η) where $y_d \sim softmax(\frac{exp(\eta_h^T \bar{z})}{\sum_{h=1}^{c-1} exp(\eta_h^T \bar{z})})$

In the sampling, index i is the number of the topic component which ranges from $1 : k$. $P(w_{dn}|\beta^d_{ni})$ in 2(b) is an exponential family distribution where i is from $1...k$. Note that now we have β^d_{ni} rather than only β^d_i since we have drawn separate distributions for each word (or feature) n.

Now, our MEDLDA-based relation-detection model can integrate diverse features of different types or the same features with different parameters.

Following the generative process, parameter estimation and inferences can be made with either Gibbs sampling or variational methods. We use variational methods since we adapt MEDLDA package[3] to mixed-membership MEDLDA and train relation detection models.

2.3 Relation Detection

With the generative process, inference and parameter estimation in place, we are ready to perform relation detection. The first step is to perform variational inference given the testing instances.

In classification, we estimate the probability of the relation type given topics and the response parameters, i.e. $p(y_d|z_{d1:dN}, \eta_{1:c-1})$. With variational approximation, we can derive the prediction rule as $F(y, z_{1:N}, \eta) = \eta^T f(y, \bar{z})$ where $f(y, \bar{z})$ is a feature vector. Now, SVM can be used to derive the

[3]this package is downloaded from http://www.cs.cmu.edu/̃junzhu/medlda.htm

prediction rule. The final prediction can be generalized exactly the same as Zhu, Ahmed and Xing (Zhu et al., 2009):

$$\hat{y} = argmax_y E[\eta^T f(y, \bar{Z})|\alpha, \beta] \quad (2)$$

3 Features

We explore the effectiveness of incorporating features into our systems as well as the baselines. For this, we construct feature sets similar to Jiang and Zhai (2007) and Zhou (2005). Three kinds of features are employed:

1. **BOW** The Bag of Words (BOW) feature captures all the words in our mini-document. It comprises of the words of the two NE mentions and the words between them.

2. **SYN** The SYN features are constructed to capture syntactic, semantic and structural information of the mini-document. They include features such as HM1 (the head word of the first mention), HM2 (the head word of the second mention), ET1, ET2, M1 and M2 (Entity types and mention types of the two mentions involved), #MB (number of other mentions in between the two mentions), #WB (number of words in between the two mentions).

3. **COMP** The COMP features are composite features that are similar to SYN, but they additionally capture language order and dependencies between the features mentioned above. These include features such as HM1HM2 (combining head word of mention 1 and head word of mention 2) , ET12 (combinations of mention entity type), ML12 (combination of mention levels), M1InM2 or M2InM1 (flag indicating whether M2/M1 is included in M1/M2).

The main intuitions behind employing composite features, COMP, are as follows. First, they capture the ordering information. The ordering of words are not captured by BOW. That is, BOW features assume exchangeability. This works for models based on random or seeded sampling (e.g. LDA) – as long as words sampled are associated with a topic, the hidden topics of the documents can be discovered. In the case of ERD, this assumption might work with symmetric relations. However, when the relations are asymmetric, ordering information is important. Composite features such as HM1HM2 encodes what mention head word precedes the other. Second, features such as M1InM2 or M2InM1 capture token dependencies. Besides exchangeability, LDA-based models also assume that words are conditionally independent. Consequently, the system cannot capture the knowledge that some mentions may be included in other mentions. By constructing features such as M1InM2 or M2InM1, we encode the dependency information explicitly.

4 Experiments

As MEDLDA is a combination of maximum margin principle with maximum likelihood estimation for topic modes, we compare it with two baseline systems. The first, *SVM*, uses only the maximum margin principle, while the second, *LLDA*, uses only maximum likelihood estimation for topic modeling.

4.1 Data

We use the ACE corpus (Phase 2, 2005) for evaluation. The ACE corpus has annotations for both entities and relations. The corpus has six major relations types, 23 subtypes and 7 entity types. In this work, we focus only on the six high-level relation types listed in Table 1. In addition to the the 6 major types, we have an additional category, no relation (NO-REL), that exists between entities that are not related.

The data for our experiments consists of pairs of NEs from a sentence, and the gold standard annotation of their relation type (or NO-REL). All relations in the ACE corpus are intra-sentential and hence we do not create NE pairs that cross sentence boundaries. Also, almost all positive instances are within two mentions of each other. Hence, we create NE pairs for only those NEs that have at most 2 intervening NEs in between. This gives us a total of 38,342 relation instances of which 32,640 are negative instances (NO-REL) and 5702 are positive relation instances belonging to one of the 6 categories.

4.2 Experimental Setup

We use 80% of the instances for training and 20% for testing. The topic numbers and the penalty parameter of the cost function C are first determined

Major Type	Definition	Example
ART artifact	User, owner, inventor or manufacturer	the makers of the Kursk
GEN-AFF	citizen, resident, religion, ethnicity and organization-location	U.S. Companies
ORG-AFF (Org-affiliation)	employment, founder, ownership, sports-affiliation, investor-shareholder student-alumni and membership	The CEO of Siemens
PART-WHOLE	geographical, subsidiary and so on	a branch of U.S bank
PER-SOC (person-social)	business, family and lasting personal relationship	a spokesman for the senator
PHYS (physical)	located or near	a military base in Germany

Table 1: Relation types for ACE 05 corpus

for each of the models (wherever applicable) using the training data. Best parameters are determined for the three conditions: 1) BOW features alone *BOW*, 2) BOW plus SYN features (*PlusSYN*) and 3) BOW plus SYN and COMP features (*PlusCOMP*). All systems achieved their overall best performance with PlusCOMP features (see Section 4.4 for a detailed analysis).

4.2.1 MEDLDA

The number of topics are determined using the equation $2K_0 + K_1$ following Zhu, Ahmed and Xing (2009) and $K_1 = 2K_0$. K_0 is the number of topics per class and K_1 is the number of topics shared by all relation types. The choice of topics is based on the intuition that the shared component K_1 should use all class labels to model common latent structure while non-overlapping components should model specific characteristics data from each class. The ratio of topics is based on the understanding that shared topics may be more than topics of each class. The specific numbers do not produce much variation in the final results. We experimented with the following number of topics: 20, 40, 70, 80, 90, 100, 110. BOW, PlusSYN, and PlusCOMP configurations obtain the best performance for 90 topics, 80 topics, and 70 topics respectively.

Since SVMs are employed in the MEDLDA implementation, we need to determine the penalty parameter of the cost function, C. We used 5 fold cross-validation to locate the parameter C. The best values for C are 25, 28, 30 respectively for BOW, PlusSYN and PlusCOMP configurations. We used a linear kernel as it is the most commonly used kernel for text classification tasks. Since MEDLDA is run by sampling, the result may be different each time. We ran it 5 times for each setting and took the average as the final results.

4.2.2 LLDA and SVM

The setting of topics for LLDA is similar to MEDLDA. As LLDA is also run by sampling, we ran it 5 times for each setting and took the average as the final results. In SVMlight, a grid search tool is provided to locate the the best value for parameter C. The best C for all three conditions was found to be 1. All other settings for the two models are similar to those of MEDLDA.

4.3 Results

	Prec%	Rec%	F%
SVM	53.2	35.2	40.3
LLDA	28.3	51.6	36.6
MEDLDA	**57.8**	**53.2**	**55.4**

Table 2: Overall performance of the 3 systems

We present the results of the three systems built using PlusCOMP, as all systems achieved their best overall performance using these features. Table 2 reports the precision, recall and Fmeasure of the three systems averaged across all 7 categories (the best numbers for each metric are highlighted in **bold**). Here we see that MEDLDA outperforms LLDA and

Labels	SVM			LLDA			MEDLDA		
	Pre%	Rec%	F%	Pre%	Rec%	F%	Pre%	Rec%	F%
ART	30	8	14	1.5	33	3	**49**	**36**	**41**
GEN-AFF	**53**	**48**	**50**	3	32	6	40	39	40
ORG-AFF	55	35	43	**59**	58	**59**	53	**59**	56
PART-WHOLE	39	08	14	31	**82**	45	**44**	52	**48**
PER-SOC	50	17	25	7	**92**	13	**73**	76	**75**
PHYS	55	35	**43**	26	**47**	33	**56**	19	29
NO-REL	**90**	**95**	**93**	70	17	27	89	91	90

Table 3: Multi-class Classification Results with PlusCOMP for SVM, LLDA and MEDLDA for the six ACE 05 categories and NO-REL

SVM across all metrics. Specifically, there is a 15 percentage point improvement in Fmeasure over the best performing baseline. This result indicates that our approach of combining topic model with max-margin learning is effective for relation detection.

Now, looking at the results for each individual relationship category (see Table 3; the best numbers for each category and metric are highlighted in **bold**) we see that the Fmeasure for MEDLDA is better than that for SVM for 4 out of the 6 ACE relation types; and better than the Fmeasure obtained by LLDA for all relation types except ORG-AFF. Specifically, comparing with the best performing baseline, MEDLDA produces a Fmeasure improvement 27 percentage points for ART, 3 percentage points for PART-WHOLE and 50 percentage points for PER-SOC. Also, for four of the six ACE relation types, MEDLDA achieves the best precision. Even in the cases where MEDLDA is not the best performer for a relation category, its performance is not very poor (unlike, for example, SVM for PART-WHOLE and LLDA for ART, respectively).

Interestingly, the NO-REL category reveals a sharp contrast in the performance of SVM and LLDA. NO-REL is a difficult, catch-all category that is a mixture of data with diverse distributions. This is a category where maximum-margin learning is more effective than maximum-likelihood estimation. Notice that MEDLDA achieves performance close to SVM for this category. This is because, even though both LLDA and MEDLDA model hidden topics and then employ discovered hidden topics to predict relation types, MEDLDA does joint inference of MLE and MME. This joint inference helps to improve the detection of NO-REL.

Finally, we also compare our system's results (using PlusCOMP features) with the results of previous research on the same corpus (Khayyamian et al., 2009). They use similar experimental settings: every pair of entities within a sentence is regarded to involve a negative relation instance unless it is annotated as positive in the corpus. A similar filter (they use a distance filter) is used to sift out unrelated negative instances. Their train/test ratio of data split is also the same as ours.

Khayyamian, Mirroshandel and Abolhassani (2009) employ state-of-art kernel methods developed by Collins and Duffy (2002) and only report Fmeasures over the six ACE relation types. For clarity, we reproduce their results in Table 4 and repeat MEDLDA Fmeasures from Table 3 in the last column. The last row (Overall) reports the macro-averages computed over all relation types for each system. Here we see that overall, MEDLDA outperforms all kernels. MEDLDA also performs better than the best kernel for four of the six relation types.

4.4 Analysis

As mentioned previously, all three systems achieved their overall best performance with PlusCOMP features. Here, we analyze if informative features are consistently useful and if the systems can harness the informative features consistently across all relation types. Figures 3, 4 and 5 illustrate the F-measures for SVM, LLDA and MEDLDA respectively for the three conditions: BOW, PlusSYN and PlusCOMP.

Labels	CD'01	AAP	AAPD	TSAAPD-0	TSAAPD-01	MEDLDA
ART%	**51**	49	50	48	47	41
GEN-AFF %	9	10	12	11	11	**40**
ORG-AFF %	43	43	43	43	45	**56**
PART-WHOLE %	30	28	29	30	28	**48**
PER-SOC %	62	58	70	63	73	**75**
PHYS %	32	**36**	29	33	33	29
Overall (Avg)	38	37	39	38	40	**48**

Table 4: F-measures for every kernel in (Khayyamian et al., 2009) and MEDLDA

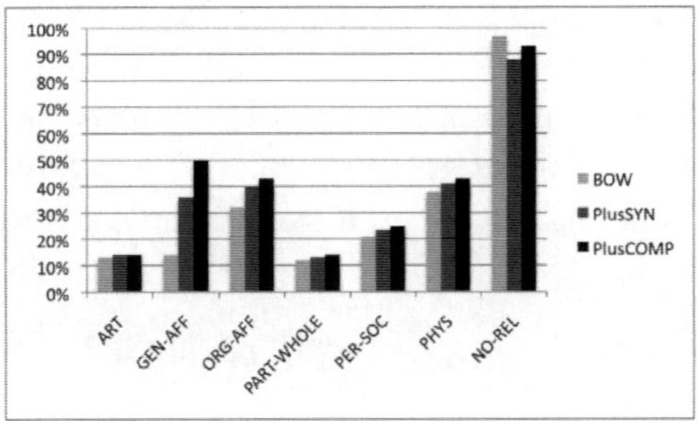

Figure 3: SVM Fmeausres for 3 feature conditions

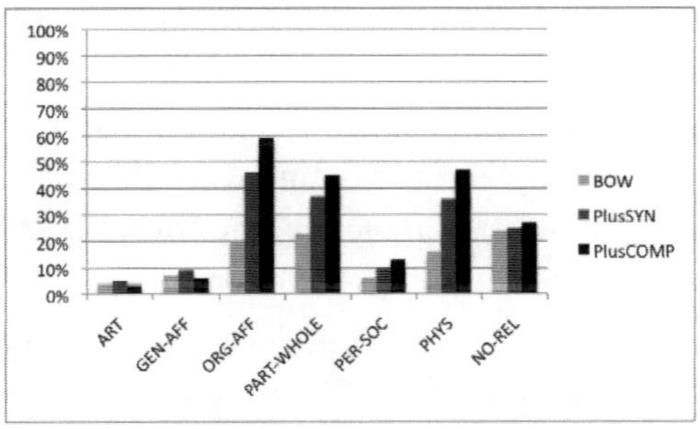

Figure 4: LLDA Fmeausres for 3 feature conditions

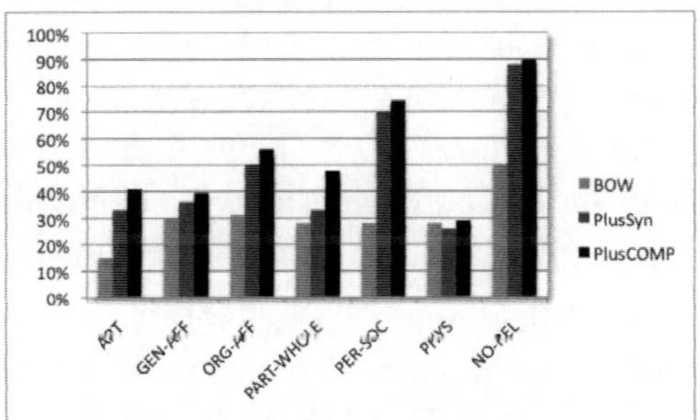

Figure 5: MEDLDA Fmeausres for 3 feature conditions

Let us first look at the best systems (based on Fmeasure) for each of the six ACE relation types in Table 3, and look at what feature set produces the best result for that system and relation. MEDLDA is the best performer for ART, PART-WHOLE and PER-SOC in Table 3. Figure 5 reveals that MEDLDA's best performance for these relation types are obtained using PlusCOMP features. Similarly SVM obtains the best Fmeasure for GEN-AFF and PHYS relations and Figure 3 shows that SVM achieves its best performance for these categories using PlusCOMP. We also see a similar trend with LLDA and the ORG-AFF relation type. These results corroborate intuition from previous research that informative features are important for relation type recognition. The only exception to this is the performance of SVM for NO-REL. This is not surprising, as the features we use are focused on determining true relation types and NO-REL is a mixture of all cases (and features) where relations do not exist.

Further analysis of the figures reveal that even though there is a general trend towards better performance with addition of more informative features, not all systems show consistent improvements across all relation types with the addition of composite features. That is, some systems get degraded performance due to feature addition. For example, in Figure 3, we see that the SVM with PlusCOMP features is outperformed by SVM with PlusSYN for ART and SVM with BOW for NO-REL. The gains from features are also inconsistent in the case of LLDA (Figure 4). While the LLDA system with PlusSYN features always improves over the one using BOW, the performance drops considerably when using PlusCOMP features for ART and GEN-AFF. On the other hand, MEDLDA (see Figure 5) shows more consistent improvement for all relation types with the addition of more complex features. Also, the gains are more substantial. This is encouraging and opens up avenues for further exploration.

5 Related Work

Previous research has explored various methods and features for relationship detection and mining. Kernel methods have been popularly used for relation detection. Some examples are are dependency tree kernels (Culotta and Sorensen, 2004), shortest dependency path kernels (Bunescu and Mooney, 2005), and more recently, convolution tree kernels (Zhao and Grishman, 2005; Zhang et al., 2006) context-sensitive convolution tree kernels (Zhou et al., 2007) and dynamic syntax tree kernels (Qian et al., 2008). Kernel methods for relation extraction focus on representing and capturing the structured information of the text between the entities. In our MEDLDA model, instead of computing distances between subtrees, we sample topics based on their distributions. The sampling is not only on the (mini) document level, but also on the word level or on the syntactic or semantic level. Our model focuses on addressing the underlying semantics more directly than typical kernel-based methods.

Chan and Roth (2011) employ constraints using an integer linear programming (ILP) framework. Using this, they apply rich linguistic and knowledge-based constraints based on coreference annotations, a hierarchy of relations, syntacto-semantic structure, and knowledge from Wikipedia. In our work, we focus on capturing the latent semantics of the text between the NEs.

A variety of features have been explored for ERD in previous research (Zhou et al., 2005; Zhou et al., 2008; Jiang and Zhai, 2007; Miller et al., 2000). Syntactic features such as POS tags and dependency path between entities; semantic features such as Word-Net relations, semantic parse trees and types of NEs; and structural features such as which entity came first in the sentence have been found useful for ERD. We too observe the utility of informative features for this task. However, exploration of the feature space is not the main focus of this work. Rather, our focus is on whether the models are capable of incorporating rich features. A fuller exploration of rich heterogeneous features is the focus of our future work.

A closely related task is that of relation mining and discovery, where unsupervised, semi-supervised approaches have been effectively employed (Hasegawa et al., 2004; Mintz et al., 2009; Jiang, 2009). For example, Hasegawa et al. (2004) use clustering and entity type information, while Mintz et al. (2009) employ distant supervision. Our ERD task is different from these as we focus on classifying the relation types into predefined relation types in the ACE05 corpus.

Topic models have been applied previously for a number of NLP tasks (e.g. (Lin et al., 2006; Titov and McDonald, 2008). LDAs have also been employed to reduce feature dimensions in relation detection systems (Hachey, 2006). However, to the best of our knowledge, this is the first work to make use of topic models to perform relation detection.

6 Conclusion and Future Work

In this work, we presented a system for entity relation detection based on mixed-membership MEDLDA. Our approach was motivated by the idea that combination of max margin and maximum likelihood can help to improve relation detection task. For this, we adapted the existing work on MEDLDA and mixed membership models and formulated ERD as a topic detection task. To the best of our knowledge, this is the first work to make full use of topic models for relation detection.

Our experiments show that the proposed approach achieves better overall performance than SVM-based and LLDA-based approaches across all metrics. We also experimented with different features and the effectiveness of the different models for harnessing these features. Our analysis show that our MEDLDA-based approach is able to effectively and consistently incorporate informative features.

As a model that incorporates maximum-likelihood, maximum-margin and mixed membership learning, MEDLDA has the potential of incorporating rich kernel functions or conditional topic random fields (CTRF) (Zhu and Xing, 2010). These are some of the promising directions for our future exploration.

References

ACE. 2000-2005. Automatic Content Extraction. *http://www.ldc.upenn.edu/Projects/ACE/*.

D.M. Blei and J. McAuliffe. 2008. Supervised topic models. *Advances in Neural Information Processing Systems*, 20:121–128.

R.C. Bunescu and R.J. Mooney. 2005. A shortest path dependency kernel for relation extraction. In *HLT & EMNLP*.

X. Carreras and L. Màrquez. 2005. Introduction to the CoNLL-2005 shared task: Semantic role labeling. In *CONLL*, pages 152–164. ACL.

Y. Chan and D. Roth. 2011. Exploiting syntactico-semantic structures for relation extraction. In *ACL*.

M. Collins and N. Duffy. 2002. Convolution kernels for natural language. *Advances in neural information processing systems*, 1:625–632.

A. Culotta and J. Sorensen. 2004. Dependency tree kernels for relation extraction. In *Proceedings of the 42nd Annual Meeting on Association for Computational Linguistics*, page 423. ACL.

G. Doddington, A. Mitchell, M. Przybocki, L. Ramshaw, S. Strassel, and R. Weischedel. 2004. The automatic content extraction (ACE) program–tasks, data, and evaluation. In *Proceedings of LREC*, volume 4, pages 837–840.

R. Farkas, V. Vincze, G. Móra, J. Csirik, and G. Szarvas. 2010. The CoNLL-2010 Shared Task: Learning to Detect Hedges and their Scope in Natural Language Text. In *CoNLL-2010*, pages 1–12.

B. Hachey. 2006. Comparison of similarity models for the relation discovery task. In *COLING & ACL 2006*, page 25.

T Hasegawa, S Sekine, and Ralph Grishman. 2004. Discovering relations among named entities from large corpora. In *42nd ACL*.

J. Jiang and C.X. Zhai. 2007. A systematic exploration of the feature space for relation extraction. In *NAACL/HLT*, pages 113–120.

J. Jiang. 2009. Multi-task transfer learning for weakly-supervised relation extraction. In *47th ACL & 4th AFNLP*, pages 1012–1020. ACL.

N. Kambhatla. 2004. Combining lexical, syntactic, and semantic features with maximum entropy models for extracting relations. In *ACL 2004 Interactive poster and demonstration sessions*.

M. Khayyamian, S.A. Mirroshandel, and H. Abolhassani. 2009. Syntactic tree-based relation extraction using a generalization of Collins and Duffy convolution tree kernel. In *HLT/NAACL,: Student Research Workshop*.

Wei-Hao Lin, Theresa Wilson, Janyce Wiebe, and Alexander Hauptmann. 2006. Which side are you on? Identifying perspectives at the document and sentence levels. In *CoNLL-2006*.

S. Miller, H. Fox, L. Ramshaw, and R. Weischedel. 2000. A novel use of statistical parsing to extract information from text. In *NAACL*.

M Mintz, S Bills, R Snow, and D Jurafsky. 2009. Distant supervision for relation extraction without labeled data. In *47th ACL & 4th AFNLP*.

US NIST. 2003. The ACE 2003 Evaluation Plan. *US National Institute for Standards and Technology (NIST)*, pages 2003–08.

L. Qian, G. Zhou, F. Kong, Q. Zhu, and P. Qian. 2008. Exploiting constituent dependencies for tree kernel-based semantic relation extraction. In *22nd ACL*.

D. Ramage, D. Hall, R. Nallapati, and C.D. Manning. 2009. Labeled LDA: A supervised topic model for credit attribution in multi-labeled corpora. In *EMNLP*.

H. Shan, A. Banerjee, and N.C. Oza. 2009. Discriminative Mixed-membership Models. In *ICDM*, pages 466–475. IEEE.

Ivan Titov and Ryan McDonald. 2008. A joint model of text and aspect ratings for sentiment summarization. In *ACL-08: HLT*.

M. Zhang, J. Zhang, J. Su, and G. Zhou. 2006. A composite kernel to extract relations between entities with both flat and structured features. In *21st ICCL & 44th ACL*.

S. Zhao and R. Grishman. 2005. Extracting relations with integrated information using kernel methods. In *43rd ACL*.

G Zhou, S. Jian, Z. Jie, and Z. Min. 2005. Exploring various knowledge in relation extraction. In *In 43rd ACL*.

G Zhou, M. Zhang, D.H. Ji, and Q Zhu. 2007. Tree kernel-based relation extraction with context-sensitive structured parse tree information. In *EMNLP/CoNLL-2007*, pages 728–736.

G.D. Zhou, M. Zhang, D.H. Ji, and Q.M. Zhu. 2008. Hierarchical learning strategy in semantic relation extraction. *Information Processing & Management*, 44(3):1008–1021.

J. Zhu and E.P. Xing. 2010. Conditional Topic Random Fields. In *ICML*. ACM.

J. Zhu, A. Ahmed, and E.P. Xing. 2009. MedLDA: maximum margin supervised topic models for regression and classification. In *ICML*, pages 1257–1264. ACM.

Nonparametric Bayesian Word Sense Induction

Xuchen Yao[1] and **Benjamin Van Durme**[1,2]
[1]Department of Computer Science
[2]Human Language Technology Center of Excellence
Johns Hopkins University

Abstract

We propose the use of a nonparametric Bayesian model, the Hierarchical Dirichlet Process (HDP), for the task of Word Sense Induction. Results are shown through comparison against Latent Dirichlet Allocation (LDA), a parametric Bayesian model employed by Brody and Lapata (2009) for this task. We find that the two models achieve similar levels of induction quality, while the HDP confers the advantage of automatically inducing a variable number of senses per word, as compared to manually fixing the number of senses *a priori*, as in LDA. This flexibility allows for the model to adapt to terms with greater or lesser polysemy, when evidenced by corpus distributional statistics. When trained on out-of-domain data, experimental results confirm the model's ability to make use of a restricted set of topically coherent induced senses, when then applied in a restricted domain.

1 Introduction

Word Sense Induction (WSI) is the task of automatically discovering latent *senses* for each word *type*, across a collection of that word's *tokens* situated in context. WSI differs from Word Sense Disambiguation (WSD) in that the task does not assume access to some prespecified sense inventory. This amounts to a clustering task: instances of a word are partitioned into the same bin based on whether a system deems them to have the same underlying meaning. A large body of related work can be found in (Schütze, 1998; Pantel and Lin, 2002; Dorow and Widdows, 2003; Purandare and Pedersen, 2004; Bordag, 2006; Niu et al., 2007; Pedersen, 2007; Brody and Lapata, 2009; Li et al., 2010; Klapaftis and Manandhar, 2010).

Brody and Lapata (2009) (B&L herein) showed that the parametric Bayesian model, Latent Dirichlet Allocation (LDA), could be successfully employed for this task, as compared to previous results published for the WSI component of SemEval-2007[1] (Agirre and Soroa, 2007). A deficiency of the LDA model for WSI is that the number of senses needs to be manually specified *a priori*, either separately for each word type, or (as done by B&L) some fixed value that is shared globally across all types.

Nonparametric methods instead have the flexibility of automatically deciding the number of sense cluters (Vlachos et al., 2009; Reisinger and Mooney, 2010). In this work we first independently verify the results of B&L, and then tackle the limitation on fixing the number of senses through the use of the Hierarchical Dirichlet Process (HDP) (Teh et al., 2006), a nonparametric Bayesian model. We show this approach leads to results of similar quality as LDA, when using a bag-of-words context model, in addition to allowing for variability in the number of senses across different words and domains. When trained on a restricted domain corpus for which manually labeled sense data was present, we verify that the model may be tuned to posit a similar number of senses as determined by human judges. When trained on a broader domain collection, we show that the number of induced senses increase, in line with the intuition that a wider set of genres should lead to a greater diversity in underlying meanings. Automatically inducing the proper number of senses has great practical implications, especially in areas that require word sense disambiguation. For instance, inducing more senses for `bank` helps to tell differ-

[1]Klapaftis and Manandhar (2010) and Brody and Lapata (2009) reported the best scores so far on this dataset.

ent word senses apart for naturally more ambiguous words, and inducing less senses for `job` helps to prevent assigning too fined-grained senses in case the same words in two similar contexts are mistakenly regarded as carrying different senses.

2 Bayesian Word Sense Induction

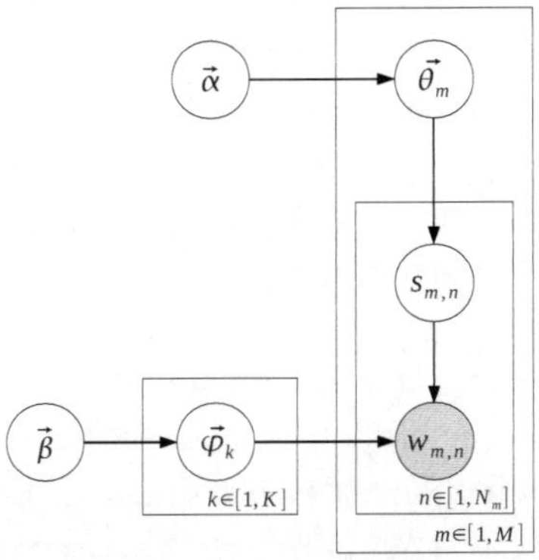

Figure 1: Latent Dirichlet Allocation (LDA) for WSI.

As in prior work including B&L, we rely on the intuition that the senses of words are hinted at by their contextual information (Yarowsky, 1992). From the perspective of a generative process, neighboring words of a target are generated by the target's underlying sense.[2]

Both LDA and HDP define graphical models that generate collections of discrete data. The sense of a target word is first drawn from a distribution and then the context of this word is generated according to that distribution. But while LDA assumes a fixed, finite set of distributions, the HDP draws from an infinite set of distributions generated by a Dirichlet Process. This section details the distinction.

Figure 1 shows the LDA model for word sense induction. The conventional notion of document is replaced by a *pseudo-document*, consisting of every word in an N_m-word window centered on the target item. $w_{m,n}$ is the n-th token of the m-th pseudo-document for target word w. $s_{m,n}$ is the corresponding sense for $w_{m,n}$. Suppose there are K senses for the target word w, then the distribution over a context word $w_{m,n}$ is:

[2]For instance, given the word `bank` with a sense `river bank`, it is more likely that the neighboring words are `river`, `lake` and `water` than `finance`, `money` and `loan`.

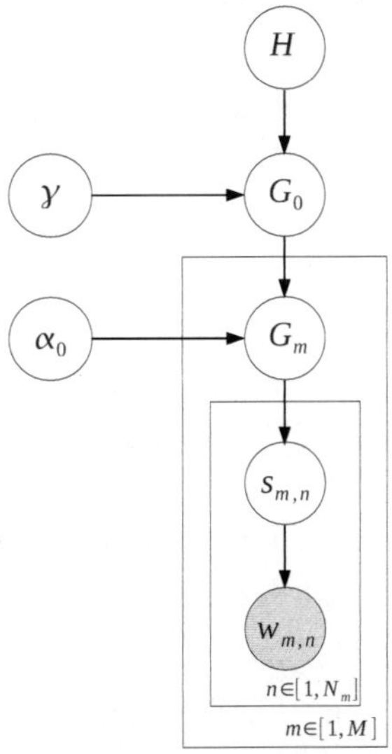

Figure 2: Hierarchical Dirichlet Process (HDP) for WSI.

$$p(w_{m,n}) = \sum_{k=1}^{K} p(w_{m,n} \mid s_{m,n} = k) p(s_{m,n} = k).$$

Let the word distribution given a sense be $p(w_{m,n} \mid s_{m,n} = k) = \vec{\varphi}_k$, which is a vector of length V (vocabulary size) that is generated from a Dirichlet distribution: $\vec{\varphi}_k \sim Dir(\vec{\beta})$. Let the sense distribution given a document be $p(s_{m,n} \mid d = m) = \vec{\theta}_m$, which is a vector of length K that is generated from a Dirichlet distribution: $\vec{\theta}_m \sim Dir(\vec{\alpha})$. The generative story for the data under LDA is then:

For $k \in (1, ..., K)$ senses:
  Sample mixture component: $\vec{\varphi}_k \sim Dir(\vec{\beta})$.
For $m \in (1, ..., M)$ pseudo-documents:
  Sample topic components $\vec{\theta}_m \sim Dir(\vec{\alpha})$.
  For $n \in (1, ..., N_m)$ words in pseudo-document m:
    Sample sense index $s_{m,n} \sim Mult(\vec{\theta}_m)$.
    Sample word $w_{m,n} \sim Mult(\vec{\varphi}_{s_{m,n}})$.

The sense distribution over a word is captured as K mixture components. In the HDP however, we assume the number of active components is unknown, and should be inferred from the data. For each pseudo-document, the sense component $s_{m,n}$ for word $w_{m,n}$ has a nonparametric prior G_m. G_m is nonparametric in the sense that for every new pseudo-document m, a new G_m is sampled from a base distribution G_0. As the corpus grows, there are more and more G_m's. However, the mixture component $s_{m,n}$, drawn from G_m, can be shared among pseudo-documents. Thus the number of senses do not simply multiply out as m grows. Both G_0 and G_m's are distributed according to a Dirichlet Process (DP) (Ferguson, 1973). The generative story is:

Select base distribution $G_0 \sim DP(\gamma, H)$ which provides an unlimited inventory of senses.
For $m \in (1, ..., M)$ pseudo-documents:
  Draw $G_m \sim DP(\alpha_0, G_0)$.
For $n \in (1, ..., N_m)$ words in pseudo-document m:
  Sample $s_{m,n} \sim G_m$.
  Sample $w_{m,n} \sim Mult(\vec{\varphi}_{s_{m,n}})$.

Hyperparameters γ and α_0 are the concentration parameters of the DP, controlling the variability of the distributions G_0 and G_m. In a Chinese restaurant franchise metaphor of the HDP, multiple restaurants (documents) share a set of dishes (senses). Then γ controls the variability of the global sense distribution and α_0 controls the variability of each customer's (word) choice of dishes (senses).[3]

3 Experiment Setting

Model B&L experimented with variations to the LDA model that allowed for generating multiple layers of features, such as smaller (5w) and larger (10w) bag-of-word contexts, and syntactic features. The additional complexity beyond the standard model led to only tenuous performance gains. Normal LDA, when trained on pseudo-documents built from 10 words of surrounding context, performed only slightly below their best reported results.[4] Especially as our goal here was to investigate the sense-specification problem, rather than eking out further improvements in the base WSI evaluation measure, we chose to compare a standard LDA model to HDP, both strictly using a 10 word context.[5]

Test Data Following B&L, we perform WSI on nouns. The evaluation data comes from the WSI task of SemEval-2007 (Agirre and Soroa, 2007). It is derived from the Wall Street Journal portion of the Penn TreeBank (Marcus et al., 1994) and contains 15,852 instances of excerpts on 35 nouns. All the nouns are hand-annotated with their OntoNotes senses (Hovy et al., 2006), with an average of 3.9 senses per word.

Evaluation Method WSI is an unsupervised task that results in sense clusters with no explicit mapping to manually annotated sense data. To derive such a mapping, we follow the *supervised evaluation* strategy of Agirre and Soroa (2007). Annotated senses from SemEval-2007 are partitioned into a standard mapping set (72%), a dev set (14%) and a test set (14%). After an WSI system has tagged the elements in the mapping set with their "cluster IDs", then a cluster to sense derivation is constructed by simply assigning to each cluster the manual sense label that has the highest in-cluster frequency. Once such a mapping has been established, then results on the dev or test set are reported based on treating cluster assignment as a WSD operation.

Training Data As out-of-domain source, we extracted 930K instances of the 35 nouns from the British National Corpus (BNC) (Clear, 1993). As in-domain source we extracted another 930K instances from WSJ in years 87/88/90/94. All pseudo-documents use the ± 10 contextual window.

4 Evaluation

We trained the LDA and HDP models on the WSJ and BNC datasets separately. In their experiments with LDA, B&L iteratively tried 3 up to 9 senses, and then reported the number that led to best results in evaluation (4 senses for WSJ, 8 for BNC). We repeated this approach for LDA, with hyper-parameters $\alpha = 0.02$ and $\beta = 0.1$. For the HDP model, we tuned hyper-parameters on the SemEval-2007 dev set.[6] See Table 1 for results, averaged over 5 runs of LDA and 3 runs of HDP.

We report several findings based on this experiment. First, for the LDA models trained on WSJ and BNC, our F1 measures are 0.8% lower than reported by B&L.[7] Second, based on our own experiment, the HDP model performance is slightly better than that of LDA when training with BNC.

[3]Gibbs sampling (Geman and Geman, 1990) can be applied for inference. Specifically, Teh et al. (2006) describes the posterior sampling in the Chinese restaurant franchise.

[4]F-score of 86.9% (10w), as compared to 87.3% (10w+5w).

[5]We relied on implementations of LDA and HDP respectively from MALLET (McCallum, 2002), and Wang (2010).

[6]Final parameters: $H = 0.1$, $\alpha_0 \sim Gamma(0.1, 0.028)$, $\gamma \sim Gamma(1, 0.1)$.

[7]We consider this acceptable experimental deviation, given the minor variation in respective training data.

WSJ		BNC	
LDA-4s*	86.9	LDA-8s*	84.6
LDA-4s	86.1	LDA-8s	83.8
HDP	86.7	HDP	$85.7^{\triangle}$

Table 1: F-measure when training with WSJ (in-domain) and BNC (out-of-domain). Results with * are taken from B&L. **4** or **8** senses were used per word. △: statistically significant against LDA-8s by paired permutation test with $p < 0.001$. The standard baseline, always picking the most frequent sense observed in training, scores 80.9.

	WSJ		BNC	
	Train	Test	Train	Test
LDA	4.0	3.9	8.0	7.4
HDP	5.8	3.9	9.4	4.6

Table 2: The average number of senses the LDA and HDP models output when training with WSJ/BNC and testing on SemEval-2007, which has 3.9 senses per word on average.

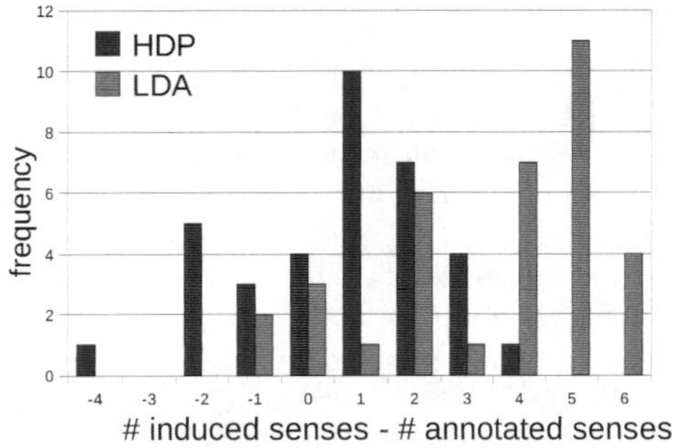

Figure 3: The difference between induced number of senses and annotated senses. The training set is BNC. The test set is SemEval-2007, containing 35 nouns with 3.9 senses. LDA induced 7.4 senses and HDP induced 4.6 senses on average.

WSJ		BNC	
LDA-5.8s	86.0	LDA-9.4s	82.7
LDA-3.9s	85.3	LDA-3.9s	81.4
HDP-5.8s	86.7	HDP-9.4s	$85.7^{\triangle}$

Table 3: F1 measure when training LDA with three other settings: 5.8s, 9.4s and 3.9s. △: statistically significant against both LDA-9.4s and LDA-3.9s (for BNC) by paired permutation test with $p < 0.001$.

Third, the HDP model appears to better adapt to data in other domains. When switching the training set from WSJ (in-domain) to BNC (out-of-domain), we, along with B&L, found a 2.3% drop with LDA models. However, with the HDP model, there is only a 1% drop in F1. Moreover, even trained on out-of-domain data, HDP can still better infer the number of senses from the test data, which is illustrated next.

Table 2 shows the number of senses induced from each dataset. When training on WSJ and test on SemEval-2007, HDP induced the correct number of senses (3.9 on average) from test, while LDA did this by assuming 4 senses from the training data. When there is a domain mismatch between training (BNC) and test (SemEval-2007, which comes from the 1989 WSJ), the LDA model preferred far more than the annotated number of senses (7.4 vs. 3.9), largely due to the fact that it assumed 8 senses during training. However, even though the HDP model induced more senses (9.4) when training on the broader coverage BNC set, it still inferred a much reduced average of 4.6 senses on test.

The BNC, being a *balanced corpus*, covers more diverse genres than the WSJ: we would expect it to lead to a more inclusive model of word sense. Figure 3 illustrates this comparison through the difference between sense numbers. For the 35 human-annotated nouns, HDP induced the number of senses mostly within an error of ± 2, whereas LDA tended to prefer $3 - 6$ more senses than recognized by annotators (on average the HDP model was off by 1.6 senses, as compared to 3.6 by LDA). Finally, the F1 performance of HDP is 1.9% better than LDA (85.7% vs. 83.8%).

We further evaluated the LDA model by training separately for each of the 35 nouns, first setting as the number of topics the amount induced by HDP (on average, 5.8/9.4 senses for WSJ/BNC), then using the number of senses as used by the human annotators in SemEval-2007 (an average of 3.8). As seen in Table 3, in each of these cases HDP remained the superior model.

5 Conclusion

We proposed the use of a nonparametric Bayesian model (HDP) for word sense induction and compared it with the parametric model by Brody and Lapata (2009), based on LDA. The HDP model confers the advantage of automatically identifying the number of senses, besides having equivalent (or better) performance than the LDA model, verified using the SemEval-2007 dataset. Future work includes large scale sense induction over a larger vocabulary, in tasks such as Paraphrase Acquisition.

References

Eneko Agirre and Aitor Soroa. 2007. Semeval-2007 Task 02: Evaluating Word Sense Induction And Discrimination Systems. In *Proceedings of the 4th International Workshop on Semantic Evaluations*, SemEval '07, pages 7–12.

Stefan Bordag. 2006. Word Sense Induction: Triplet-Based Clustering And Automatic Evaluation. In *Proceedings of the 11th EACL*, pages 137–144.

Samuel Brody and Mirella Lapata. 2009. Bayesian Word Sense Induction. In *EACL '09: Proceedings of the 12th Conference of the European Chapter of the Association for Computational Linguistics*, pages 103–111.

Jeremy H. Clear, 1993. *The British national corpus*, pages 163–187. MIT Press, Cambridge, MA, USA.

Beate Dorow and Dominic Widdows. 2003. Discovering Corpus-Specific Word Senses. In *Proceedings of the tenth conference on European chapter of the Association for Computational Linguistics*, EACL '03, pages 79–82.

T. S. Ferguson. 1973. A Bayesian Analysis of Some Nonparametric Problems. *The Annals of Statistics*, 1(2):209–230.

S. Geman and D. Geman, 1990. *Stochastic Relaxation, Gibbs Distributions, And The Bayesian Restoration Of Images*, pages 452–472.

Eduard Hovy, Mitchell Marcus, Martha Palmer, Lance Ramshaw, and Ralph Weischedel. 2006. OntoNotes: the 90% solution. In *Proceedings of the Human Language Technology Conference of the NAACL, Companion Volume: Short Papers*, NAACL-Short '06, pages 57–60.

Ioannis Klapaftis and Suresh Manandhar. 2010. Word Sense Induction & Disambiguation Using Hierarchical Random Graphs. In *Proceedings of the 2010 Conference on Empirical Methods in Natural Language Processing*, pages 745–755, October.

Linlin Li, Benjamin Roth, and Caroline Sporleder. 2010. Topic Models For Word Sense Disambiguation And Token-Based Idiom Detection. In *Proceedings of the 48th Annual Meeting of the Association for Computational Linguistics*, ACL '10, pages 1138–1147.

Mitchell P. Marcus, Beatrice Santorini, and Mary A. Marcinkiewicz. 1994. Building a Large Annotated Corpus of English: The Penn Treebank. *Computational Linguistics*, 19(2):313–330.

Andrew Kachites McCallum. 2002. MALLET: A Machine Learning for Language Toolkit.

Zheng-Yu Niu, Dong-Hong Ji, and Chew-Lim Tan. 2007. I2R: Three Systems For Word Sense Discrimination, Chinese Word Sense Disambiguation, And English Word Sense Disambiguation. In *Proceedings of the 4th International Workshop on Semantic Evaluations*, SemEval '07, pages 177–182.

Patrick Pantel and Dekang Lin. 2002. Discovering Word Senses From Text. In *Proceedings of the eighth ACM SIGKDD international conference on Knowledge discovery and data mining*, KDD '02, pages 613–619.

Ted Pedersen. 2007. UMND2: SenseClusters applied to the sense induction task of Senseval-4. In *Proceedings of the 4th International Workshop on Semantic Evaluations*, SemEval '07, pages 394–397.

Amruta Purandare and Ted Pedersen. 2004. Word Sense Discrimination by Clustering Contexts in Vector and Similarity Spaces. In *Proceedings of CoNLL-2004*, pages 41–48.

Joseph Reisinger and Raymond J. Mooney. 2010. A Mixture Model with Sharing for Lexical Semantics. In *Proceedings of the Conference on Empirical Methods in Natural Language Processing (EMNLP-2010)*, pages 1173–1182, MIT, Massachusetts, USA.

Hinrich Schütze. 1998. Automatic Word Sense Discrimination. *Comput. Linguist.*, 24:97–123, March.

Y. W. Teh, M. I. Jordan, M. J. Beal, and D. M. Blei. 2006. Hierarchical Dirichlet Processes. *Journal of the American Statistical Association*, 101(476):1566–1581.

Andreas Vlachos, Anna Korhonen, and Zoubin Ghahramani. 2009. Unsupervised and constrained Dirichlet process mixture models for verb clustering. In *Proceedings of the Workshop on Geometrical Models of Natural Language Semantics*, GEMS '09, pages 74–82.

Chong Wang. 2010. An implementation of hierarchical dirichlet process (HDP) with split-merge operations.

David Yarowsky. 1992. Word-Sense Disambiguation Using Statistical Models Of Roget's Categories Trained On Large Corpora. In *Proceedings of the 14th conference on Computational linguistics*, pages 454–460.

Invariants and Variability of Synonymy Networks: Self Mediated Agreement by Confluence

Benoît Gaillard
CLLE-ERSS, CNRS
University of Toulouse
Toulouse, France
benoit.gaillard@univ-tlse2.fr

Bruno Gaume
CLLE-ERSS, CNRS
University of Toulouse
Toulouse, France
bruno.gaume@univ-tlse2.fr

Emmanuel Navarro
IRIT
University of Toulouse
Toulouse, France
navarro@irit.fr

Abstract

Edges of graphs that model real data can be seen as judgements whether pairs of objects are in relation with each other or not. So, one can evaluate the similarity of two graphs with a measure of agreement between judges classifying pairs of vertices into two categories (connected or not connected). When applied to synonymy networks, such measures demonstrate a surprisingly low agreement between various resources of the same language. This seems to suggest that the judgements on synonymy of lexemes of the same lexicon radically differ from one dictionary editor to another. In fact, even a strong disagreement between edges does not necessarily mean that graphs model a completely different reality: although their edges seem to disagree, synonymy resources may, at a coarser grain level, outline similar semantics. To investigate this hypothesis, we relied on shared common properties of real world data networks to look at the graphs at a more global level by using random walks. They enabled us to reveal a much better agreement between dense zones than between edges of synonymy graphs. These results suggest that although synonymy resources may disagree at the level of judgements on single pairs of words, they may nevertheless convey an essentially similar semantic information.

1 Introduction

More and more resources exist, built with various approaches and methods and with many different aims and intended uses. A new issue raised by this growth is that of comparing various resources. A lexical resource is usually based on semantic judgements about lexical elements (a human judgement performed by a lexicographer, or a machine-based judgement in the case of automatically built resources). Often, two independently built resources that describe the same linguistic reality only show a weak agreement even when based on human judgements under the same protocol (Murray and Green, 2004).

Many of such resources, such as WordNet (Fellbaum, 1998) or Wiktionary[1] (Zesch et al., 2008; Sajous et al., 2010) can be modelled as graphs. A graph encodes a binary relation on a set V of vertices. A graph $G = (V, E)$ is therefore defined by a finite, non empty set of $n = |V|$ vertices and by a set $E \subseteq V \times V$ of $m = |E|$ couples of vertices (edges). In the linguistic field, vertices can be various elements of the lexicon: lemmas, word senses, syntactic frames... and edges can describe various relations: synonymy, hyperonymy, translation, cooccurrence... Edges between two vertices can be seen as judgements that decide whether the considered relation applies to this pair. For example, in a synonymy graph, an edge exists between two words if they were judged to be synonyms by the lexicographer who was compiling the dictionary. So, different graphs that model dictionaries of synonyms are built according to the judgements of various "judges".

We first illustrate, in section 2, how various standard synonymy resources of English and French share common structural properties: they all are Hierarchical Small Worlds (HSW). However, we then

[1] http://www.wiktionary.org/

show that the synonymy judgements they describe seem to disagree: the Kappa (Cohen, 1960) between the edges of any two such resources remains surprisingly low. In the third section, we analyse this apparent disagreement and in section 4, we address it by proposing an alternative view of the networks, based on random walks. This more global view enables us to assess if disagreeing synonymy networks nevertheless concord at a more global level, because they model the same linguistic reality. Beyond the usual Kappa agreement measure, which is based on the local comparison of two category judgements (a pair is or is not a pair of synonyms), we can show that synonymy judgements do not essentially diverge on the lexical semantic structure that emerges from them. In the fifth section, we conclude by outlining possible applications and perspectives of this work.

2 Graph modelling of various synonymy resources

In order to study the similarities and variations of lexical resources, let us study a sample of graphs that model several standard synonymy resources. We analyse five standard, general purpose, paper dictionaries of French synonyms[2]: Bailly (Bai), Benac (Ben), Bertaud du Chazaut (Ber), Larousse (Lar), Robert (Rob). We also study synonymy relations extracted from the Princeton Word Net (PWN) and from the English Wiktionary (Wik). The PWN synonymy network was built according to the following rule: an edge is drawn between any two words that belong to the same synset. The Wiktionary synonymy network was extracted from Wiktionary dumps[3] by methods exposed in (Sajous et al., 2010). Each of these resources is split[4] by parts of speech (Nouns, Verbs, Adjectives) resulting in three different synonymy graphs, designated, for example for the Robert dictionary, as follows: Rob_N, Rob_V, Rob_A.

[2]Synonymy relations from each of these dictionaries were extracted by the INALF/ATILF Research Unit and corrected by the CRISCO Research Unit.

[3]http://redac.univ-tlse2.fr/lexiques/wiktionaryx.html

[4]Note that splitting is not necessary. The following work would apply similarly to whole resources.

2.1 Invariants : similar structural properties

Most lexical networks, as most field networks[5], are Hierarchical Small World (HSW) Networks that share similar properties (Watts and Strogatz, 1998; Albert and Barabasi, 2002; Newman, 2003; Gaume et al., 2010; Steyvers and Tenenbaum, 2005). They exhibit a **low density** (not many edges), **short paths** (the average number of edges L on the shortest path between two vertices is low), a high **clustering rate** C (locally densely connected subgraphs can be found whereas the whole graph is globally sparse in edges), and the distribution of their degrees follows a **power law**. All graphs in our sample exhibit the HSW properties. For example, Table 1 shows the pedigrees of synonymy graphs of verbs(for space reasons we only show results for verbs, results are similar for the two other parts of speech). In this table, n and m are the number of vertices and edges, $\langle k \rangle$ is the average degree of vertices, and λ is the coefficient of the power law that fits the distribution of degrees, with a correlation coefficient r^2. n_{lcc} and L_{lcc} are the number of vertices and the average path length measured on the largest connected component. Even if n and $\langle k \rangle$ vary across dictionaries, L_{lcc} is always small, C is always higher than for equivalent random graphs (Newman, 2003) and the distribution of degrees remains close to a power law with a good correlation coefficient.

Table 1: Pedigrees of seven synonymy graphs (verbs).

	n	m	$\langle k \rangle$	n_{lcc}	m_{lcc}	C	L_{lcc}	λ	r^2
Bai_V	3082	3648	2.46	2774	3417	0.04	8.24	-2.33	0.94
Ben_V	3549	4680	2.73	3318	4528	0.03	6.52	-2.10	0.96
Ber_V	6561	25177	7.71	6524	25149	0.13	4.52	-1.88	0.93
Lar_V	5377	22042	8.44	5193	21926	0.17	4.61	-1.94	0.88
Rob_V	7357	26567	7.48	7056	26401	0.12	4.59	-2.01	0.93
PWN_V	11529	23019	6.3	6534	20806	0.47	5.9	-2.4	0.90
Wik_V	7339	8353	2.8	4285	6093	0.11	8.9	-2.4	0.94

2.2 Variability : a low agreement between edges

Although all these graphs are HSW, Table 1 shows that the lexical coverage (n) and the number of synonymy links (m) significantly vary across graphs. Given two graphs $G_1 = (V_1, E_1)$ and $G_2 =$

[5]Field networks are networks that model real data gathered by field work, for example in sociology, linguistics or biology. They contrast with artificial networks (deterministic or random).

(V_2, E_2), in order to compare their lexical coverages, we compute the Recall ($R_\bullet$), Precision ($P_\bullet$) and F-score ($F_\bullet$) of their vertex sets:

$$R_\bullet(G_1, G_2) = \frac{|V_1 \cap V_2|}{|V_2|} \quad P_\bullet(G_1, G_2) = \frac{|V_1 \cap V_2|}{|V_1|}$$

$$F_\bullet(G_1, G_2) = 2.\frac{R_\bullet(G_1,G_2).P_\bullet(G_1,G_2)}{R_\bullet(G_1,G_2)+P_\bullet(G_1,G_2)}$$

F-scores of pairs of comparable graphs (same language and same part of speech) of our sample remain moderate. Table 2 illustrates these measures on the eleven pairs of graphs involving the five French synonymy graphs (verbs) and the two English ones. It shows that the lexical coverages of the various synonymy graphs do not perfectly overlap.

Table 2: Precision, Recall and F-score of vertex sets of eleven pairs of graphs. G_1 in rows, G_2 in cols.

		Ben_V	Ber_V	Lar_V	Rob_V	Wik_V
Bai_V	$R_\bullet$	0.66	0.45	0.51	0.40	
	$P_\bullet$	0.76	0.96	0.90	0.95	
	$F_\bullet$	0.71	0.61	0.65	0.56	
Ben_V	$R_\bullet$		0.52	0.58	0.45	
	$P_\bullet$		0.96	0.88	0.93	
	$F_\bullet$		0.68	0.70	0.60	
Ber_V	$R_\bullet$			0.85	0.73	
	$P_\bullet$			0.70	0.82	
	$F_\bullet$			0.77	0.77	
Lar_V	$R_\bullet$				0.68	
	$P_\bullet$				0.92	
	$F_\bullet$				0.78	
PWN_V	$R_\bullet$					0.49
	$P_\bullet$					0.31
	$F_\bullet$					0.38

The value of $F_\bullet(G_1, G_2)$ measures the relative lexical coverage of G_1 and G_2 but does not evaluate the agreement between the synonymy judgements modelled by the graphs' edges. The Kappa of Cohen (Cohen, 1960) is a common measure of agreement between different judges who categorize the same set of objects. In the case of graphs, the judgements are not applied to simple entities but to relations between pairs of entities. Two synonymy graphs $G_1 = (V_1, E_1)$ and $G_2 = (V_2, E_2)$ give two judgements on pairs of vertices. For example, if a pair $(u, v) \in V_1 \times V_1$ is judged as synonymous then $(u, v) \in E_1$, else $(u, v) \in \overline{E_1}$. To measure the agreement between edges of G_1 and G_2, one first has to reduce the two graphs to their common vertices:

- $G'_1 = \big(V' = (V_1 \cap V_2), E'_1 = E_1 \cap (V' \times V')\big)$;
- $G'_2 = \big(V' = (V_1 \cap V_2), E'_2 = E_2 \cap (V' \times V')\big)$;

For each pair of vertices $(a, b) \in (V' \times V')$, four cases are possible:

- $(a, b) \in E'_1 \bigcap E'_2$: agreement on pair (a, b), (a, b) is synonymous for G'_1 and for G'_2;
- $(a, b) \in \overline{E'_1} \bigcap \overline{E'_2}$: agreement on pair (a, b), (a, b) is neither synonymous for G'_1 nor for G'_2;
- $(a, b) \in E'_1 \bigcap \overline{E'_2}$: disagreement on pair (a, b), (a, b) is synonymous for G'_1 but not for G'_2;
- $(a, b) \in \overline{E'_1} \bigcap E'_2$: disagreement on pair (a, b), (a, b) is synonymous for G'_2 but not for G'_1;

The agreement between the two synonymy judgements of G_1 and G_2 is measured by $K_\updownarrow(G'_1, G'_2)$, the Kappa between the two sets of edges E'_1 and E'_2:

$$K_\updownarrow(G'_1, G'_2) = \frac{(p_0 - p_e)}{(1 - p_e)} \tag{1}$$

where:

$$p_0 = \frac{1}{\omega}.(|E'_1 \cap E'_2| + |\overline{E'_1} \cap \overline{E'_2}|) \tag{2}$$

is the relative observed agreement between vertex pairs of G'_1 and vertex pairs of G'_2, where ω is the number of possible edges[6] $\omega = \frac{1}{2}.|V'|.(|V'| - 1)$.

$$p_e = \frac{1}{\omega^2}.(|E'_1|.|E'_2| + |\overline{E'_1}|.|\overline{E'_2}|) \tag{3}$$

is the hypothetical probability of chance agreement, assuming that judgements are independent[7].

The value of agreement on synonymy judgements $K_\updownarrow(G'_1, G'_2)$ varies significantly across comparable dictionary pairs of our sample, however it remains quite low. For example: $K_\updownarrow(Rob'_V, Lar'_V) = 0.518$ and $K_\updownarrow(PWN'_V, Wik'_V) = 0.247$ (cf. Table 3). On the whole sample studied in this work this agreement value ranges from 0.25 to 0.63 averaging to 0.39. This shows that, although standard dictionaries of synonyms show similar structural properties, they considerably disagree on which pairs of words are synonymous.

[6] Here, we do not consider reflexivity edges, that link vertices to themselves, as they are obviously in agreement across graphs and are not informative synonymy judgements.

[7] Note that $K_\updownarrow(G'_1, G'_2) = K_\updownarrow(G'_2, G'_1)$.

3 Analysis of the disagreement between synonymy networks

When comparing two lexical resources built by lexicographers, one can be surprised to find such a level of disagreement on synonymy relations. This divergence in judgements can be explained by editorial policies and choices (regarding, for example printed size constraints, targeted audiences...). Furthermore, lexicographers also have their subjectivity. Since synonymy is more a continuous gradient than a discrete choice (Edmonds and Hirst, 2002), an alternative limited to *synonym/not synonym* leaves ample room for subjective interpretation. However, these justifications do not account for such discrepancies between resources describing the semantic relations of words of the same language. Therefore, we expect that, if two words are deemed not synonyms in one resource G_1, but synonyms in another G_2, they will nevertheless share many neighbours in G_1 and G_2. In other words they will belong to the same dense zones. Consequently the dense zones (or clusters) found in G_1 will be similar to those found in G_2. Random walks are an efficient way to reveal these dense zones (Gaume et al., 2010). So, to evaluate the hypothesis, let us begin by studying the similarity of random walks on various synonymy networks.

3.1 Random walks on synonymy networks

If $G = (V, E)$ is a reflexive and undirected graph, let us define $d_G(u) = |\{v \in V/(u, v) \in E\}|$ the degree of vertex u in graph G, and let us imagine a walker wandering on the graph G:

- At a time $t \in \mathbb{N}$, the walker is on one vertex $u \in V$;
- At time $t + 1$, the walker can reach any neighbouring vertex of u, with uniform probability.

This process is called a simple random walk (Bollobas, 2002). It can be defined by a Markov chain on V with a $n \times n$ transition matrix $[G]$:

$$[G] = (g_{u,v})_{u,v \in V}$$

$$\text{with } g_{u,v} = \begin{cases} \dfrac{1}{d_G(u)} & \text{if } (u,v) \in E, \\ 0 \text{ else.} \end{cases}$$

Since G is reflexive, each vertex has at least one neighbour (itself) thus $[G]$ is well defined. Furthermore, by construction, $[G]$ is a stochastic matrix: $\forall u \in V, \sum_{v \in V} g_{u,v} = 1$.

The probability $P^t_G(u \rightsquigarrow v)$ of a walker starting on vertex u to reach a vertex v after t steps is:

$$P^t_G(u \rightsquigarrow v) = ([G]^t)_{u,v} \tag{4}$$

One can then prove (Gaume, 2004), with the Perron-Frobenius theorem (Stewart, 1994), that if G is connected[8] (i.e. there is always at least one path between any two vertices), reflexive and undirected, then $\forall u, v \in V$:

$$\lim_{t \to \infty} P^t_G(u \rightsquigarrow v) = \lim_{t \to \infty} ([G]^t)_{u,v} = \frac{d_G(v)}{\sum_{x \in V} d_G(x)} \tag{5}$$

It means that when t tends to infinity, the probability of being on a vertex v at time t does not depend on the starting vertex but only on the degree of v. In the following we will refer to this limit as $\pi_G(v)$.

3.2 Confluence in synonymy networks

The dynamics of the convergence of random walks towards the limit (Eq. (5)) is heavily dependent on the starting node. Indeed, the trajectory of the random walker is completely governed by the topology of the graph: after t steps, any vertex v located at a distance of t links or less can be reached. The probability of this event depends on the number of paths between u and v, and on the structure of the graph around the intermediary vertices along those paths. The more interconnections between the vertices, the higher the probability of reaching v from u.

For example, if we take $G_1 = Rob_V$ and $G_2 = Lar_V$, and choose the three vertices u = *éplucher (peel)*, r = *dépecer (tear apart)* and s = *sonner (ring)*, which are such that:

- u= *éplucher (peel)* and r= *dépecer (tear apart)* are synonymous in Rob_V: $(u, r) \in E_1$;
- u= *éplucher (peel)* and r= *dépecer (tear apart)* are not synonymous in Lar_V: $(u, r) \notin E_2$;
- r= *dépecer (tear apart)* and s= *sonner (ring)* have the same number of synonyms in G_1 : $d_{G_1}(r) = d_{G_1}(s) = d_1$;

[8]The graph needs to be connected for Eq. 5 to be valid but, in practice, the work presented here also holds on disconnected graphs.

- $r=$ *dépecer (tear apart)* and $s=$ *sonner (ring)* have the same number of synonyms in G_2 : $d_{G_2}(r) = d_{G_2}(s) = d_2$.

Then Equation (5) states that $(P^t_{G_1}(u{\rightsquigarrow}r))_{1\le t}$ and $(P^t_{G_1}(u{\rightsquigarrow}s))_{1\le t}$ converge to the same limit:

$$\pi_{G_1}(r) = \pi_{G_1}(s) = \frac{d_1}{\sum_{x\in V_1} d_{G_1}(x)}$$

as do $(P^t_{G_2}(u{\rightsquigarrow}r))_{1\le t}$ and $(P^t_{G_2}(u{\rightsquigarrow}s))_{1\le t}$:

$$\pi_{G_2}(r) = \pi_{G_2}(s) = \frac{d_2}{\sum_{x\in V_2} d_{G_2}(x)}$$

However the two series do not converge with the same dynamics. At the beginning of the walk, for t small, one can expect that $P^t_{G_1}(u{\rightsquigarrow}r) > P^t_{G_1}(u{\rightsquigarrow}s)$ and $P^t_{G_2}(u{\rightsquigarrow}r) > P^t_{G_2}(u{\rightsquigarrow}s)$ because *éplucher* is semantically closer to *dépecer* than to *sonner*. Indeed the number of short paths between *éplucher* and *dépecer* is much greater than between *éplucher* and *sonner*.

Figure 1(a) shows the values of $P^t_{G_1}(u{\rightsquigarrow}r)$ and $P^t_{G_1}(u{\rightsquigarrow}s)$ versus t, and compares them to their common limit. Figure 1(b) shows the values of $P^t_{G_2}(u{\rightsquigarrow}r)$ and $P^t_{G_2}(u{\rightsquigarrow}s)$ versus t, and compares them to their common limit. These figures confirm our intuition that, since *éplucher (peel)* and *dépecer (tear apart)* are semantically close, $P^t_{G_1}(u{\rightsquigarrow}r)$ and $P^t_{G_2}(u{\rightsquigarrow}r)$ decrease to their limit. We call this phenomenon *strong confluence*. It is worth noting that this remains true even if *éplucher (peel)* and *dépecer (tear apart)* are **not** synonyms in Lar_V. Conversely, since *éplucher (peel)* and *sonner (ring)* are semantically distant, $P^t_{G_1}(u{\rightsquigarrow}s)$ and $P^t_{G_2}(u{\rightsquigarrow}s)$ increase to their asymptotic value. We call this phenomenon *weak confluence*.

3.3 Correlation of the confluence of disagreeing synonymy pairs

When two graphs G_1 and G_2 disagree on a pair of vertices (a, b) (a is a neighbour of b in one graph but not in the other) there are three possible cases for the strength of the confluence between vertices a and b:

(1) strong in both graphs (confluence agreement),

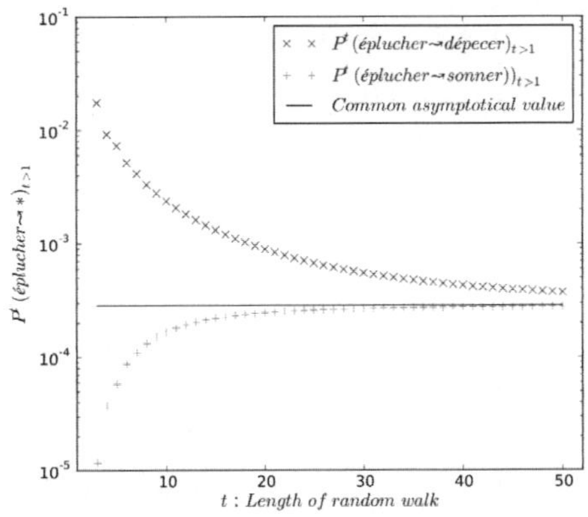

(a) $G_1 = Rob_V$

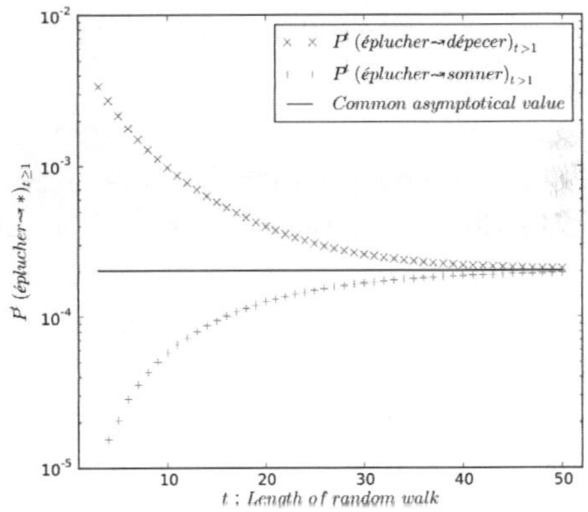

(b) $G_2 = Lar_V$

Figure 1: Confluences between *éplucher (peel)*, *dépecer (tear apart)* and *éplucher (peel)*, *sonner (ring)* in Rob_V and Lar_V.

(2) weak in both graphs (confluence agreement),

(3) strong in one graph, but weak in the other (confluence disagreement).

To contrast cases (1) and (2) from case (3) we measure the correlation between the confluences of disagreeing pairs of two synonymy networks G'_1 and G'_2. We compare it to this same correlation on two reflexive and undirected *random* graphs $R_{G'_1} = (V', E^R_1)$ and $R_{G'_2} = (V', E^R_2)$ built such that:

$$|E^R_1 \cap E^R_2| = |E'_1 \cap E'_2|,$$

$$|E^R_1 \cap \overline{E^R_2}| = |E'_1 \cap \overline{E'_2}|,$$

$$|\overline{E^R_1} \cap E^R_2| = |\overline{E'_1} \cap E'_2|,$$

which means that the Kappa agreement between $R_{G'_1}$ and $R_{G'_2}$ is the same as between G'_1 and G'_2.

For a given $t > 1$ and a set of vertex pairs $X \subseteq V' \times V'$, the correlation of confluences $\Gamma_X(G'_1, G'_2)$ is defined by the Pearson's linear correlation coefficient of the two value tables $\left(P^t_{G'_1}(u \rightsquigarrow v)\right)_{(u,v)\in X}$ and $\left(P^t_{G'_2}(u \rightsquigarrow v)\right)_{(u,v)\in X}$.

For all comparable pairs of our sample, we see that disagreeing pairs tend to have a much higher correlation of confluence than disagreeing pairs of equivalent random networks. As an example, for $G_1 = Rob_V$, $G_2 = Lar_V$ and $t = 3$, we have $\Gamma_{E'_1 \cap \overline{E'_2}}(G'_1, G'_2) = 0.41$ and $\Gamma_{\overline{E'_1} \cap E'_2}(G'_1, G'_2) = 0.38$, whereas in the case of the equivalent random graphs the same figures are close to zero.

This suggests that even if graphs disagree on the synonymy of a significant number of pairs, they nevertheless generally agree on the strength of their confluence. In other words, occurrences of cases (1) and (2) are the majority whereas occurrences of case (3) are rare. We propose in the next section an experiment to verify if we can rely on confluence to find a greater agreement between two graphs that disagree at the level of synonymy links.

4 Self mediated agreement by confluence

4.1 Hypothesis: Conciliation reveals structural similarity beyond disagreement of local synonymy

We saw in section 2.2 that the rate of agreement between edges of two standard synonymy networks G'_1 and G'_2, $K_{\updownarrow}(G'_1, G'_2)$, is usually low. However, we have noticed in Section 3.3 that the confluences of pairs on which synonymy graphs disagree are significantly more correlated ($\Gamma \approx 0.4$) than the confluence of equivalent random networks ($\Gamma \approx 0$). This suggests the following hypothesis: synonymy networks are in agreement at a level that is not taken into account by the Kappa measure on edges.

To verify this hypothesis, we try to make each pair of graphs conciliate on the basis of confluence values. We propose a conciliation process by which a graph can accept the addition of another's edges if they do not contradict its structure (i.e. there is a strong confluence value). We then assess if a strong agreement is found between the two resulting graphs.

Let $G_1 = (V_1, E_1)$ and $G_2 = (V_2, E_2)$ be two synonymy networks, both reflexive, undirected, connected, and a given $t \in \mathbb{N}^*$. We define:

- $G'_1 = \left(V' = (V_1 \cap V_2), E'_1 = E_1 \cap (V' \times V')\right)$
- $G'_2 = \left(V' = (V_1 \cap V_2), E'_2 = E_2 \cap (V' \times V')\right)$
- $G_1^{(+G_2)} = (V', E_1^+ = E'_1 \cup C_1)$ where

$$C_1 = \left\{(u,r) \in \overline{E'_1} \cap E'_2 \backslash P^t_{G'_1}(u \rightsquigarrow r) > \pi_{G'_1}(r)\right\} \quad (6)$$

- $G_2^{(+G_1)} = (V', E_2^+ = E'_2 \cup C_2)$ where

$$C_2 = \left\{(u,r) \in E'_1 \cap \overline{E'_2} \backslash P^t_{G'_2}(u \rightsquigarrow r) > \pi_{G'_2}(r)\right\} \quad (7)$$

$G_1^{(+G_2)}$ and $G_2^{(+G_1)}$ are called *accommodating graphs*. The construction of the accommodating graphs may be metaphorically understood as a conciliation protocol by which two graphs accept proposals of the other that they can reconsider. For example, $G_1^{(+G_2)}$ is the graph G'_1 enriched by edges (u, r) of G'_2 such that there is a *strong confluence* between vertices u and r in G'_1

The following property is worth noticing:

Proposition 1. *$\forall t \in \mathbb{N}^*$:*

$$(E'_1 \cap E'_2) \subseteq (E_1^+ \cap E_2^+) \subseteq (E'_1 \cup E'_2) \quad (8)$$

Proof. By definition, $E_1^+ = E'_1 \cup C_1$ and $E_2^+ = E'_2 \cup C_2$, thus $(E'_1 \cap E'_2) \subseteq (E_1^+ \cap E_2^+)$, furthermore, by definition, $C_1 \subseteq \overline{E'_1} \cap E'_2$ and $C_2 \subseteq E'_1 \cap \overline{E'_2}$ thus $(E_1^+ \cap E_2^+) \subseteq (E'_1 \cup E'_2)$. □

4.2 Experimental protocol

If, for any (G_1, G_2) synonymy resources of the same language, $K_{\updownarrow}(G_1^{(+G_2)}, G_2^{(+G_1)})$ is significantly greater than $K_{\updownarrow}(G'_1, G'_2)$, then the hypothesis is verified. The conciliation process depends on confluence measures that depend on a given t, the number of steps of the random walk. For $t = 1$, only vertices in the neighbourhood of the starting vertex are reachable. Consequently only pairs of vertices that are edges have a non null confluence. Thus $K_{\updownarrow}(G_1^{(+G_2)}, G_2^{(+G_1)}) = K_{\updownarrow}(G'_1, G'_2)$ which does not help us to contrast conciliated graphs from initial binary synonymy graphs. So we fix $t = 2$ the shortest walk length that still yields informative results.

We propose a control experiment that consists in applying the conciliation process to random networks that have the same Kappa as the pairs of synonymy networks. The construction of these random graphs is described above, in section 3.3. We measure the agreement after conciliation of 20 different random graphs. With this control experiment we assess that the observed results are specific to graphs describing the same resource, and not a mere bias of the protocol (let us imagine a protocol whereby one would add all the disagreeing edges to the graphs: not only the Kappa of the pseudo accommodating synonymy graphs would be equal to one, but also the Kappa of pseudo accommodating random graphs, which would disqualify the protocol).

4.3 Results

Table 3 summarizes Kappa and conciliated Kappa values on the pairs of synonymy graphs of verbs. It shows a significant improvement of agreement after conciliation. For example, from a moderate Kappa (0.518) between graphs Rob'_V and Lar'_V (constructed by experts), the conciliation process leads to an excellent Kappa (0.852). Conversely the random networks only increase their agreement by 0.01 (with a very low standard deviation $\sigma < 0.001$). In English, from a poor (0.247) Kappa between PWN'_V (constructed by experts) and Wik'_V (constructed by the "crowds"), the conciliation process leads to a moderate Kappa (0.530), whereas the random networks only marginally increase their agreement (0.004).

Results are similar for other parts of speech. This means that the conciliation process significantly improves the agreement between resources, even if they are originally significantly diverge.

It is interesting to notice that the most similar pairs in terms of edge agreement do not necessarily produce the most agreeing pairs of accommodating graphs. For example, the pair(Bai_V, Rob_V) agrees more than the pair (Bai_V, Lar_V), whereas for their accommodating graphs, the pair($Bai_V^{(+Rob_V)}$, $Rob_V^{(+Bai_V)}$) agrees less than the pair ($Bai_V^{(+Lar_V)}$, $Lar_V^{(+Bai_V)}$).

Table 3: Kappa (ori.) and accommodating Kappa (**acc.**) values between French and English synonymy graphs (of verbs), compared with the Kappa values between pairs of equivalent random graphs ("ori. r." and "acc. r.").

	$K_{\updownarrow}$	Ben_V	Ber_V	Lar_V	Rob_V	Wik_V
Bai_V	ori.	0.583	0.309	0.255	0.288	
	acc.	**0.777**	**0.572**	**0.603**	**0.567**	
	ori. r.	0.583	0.309	0.256	0.288	
	acc. r.	0.585	0.313	0.262	0.293	
Ben_V	ori.		0.389	0.276	0.293	
	acc.		**0.657**	**0.689**	**0.636**	
	ori. r.		0.390	0.276	0.294	
	acc. r.		0.392	0.283	0.301	
Ber_V	ori.			0.416	0.538	
	acc.			**0.838**	**0.868**	
	ori. r.			0.417	0.539	
	acc. r.			0.434	0.549	
Lar_V	ori.				0.518	
	acc.				**0.852**	
	ori. r.				0.518	
	acc. r.				0.529	
PWN_V	ori.					0.247
	acc.					**0.540**
	ori. r.					0.247
	acc. r.					0.251

So, when G_1 and G_2 are two synonymy graphs of a given language, then they are able to address their local synonymy disagreement and to reach a significantly better agreement. On the other hand, the agreement of random networks does not really improve after conciliation. This proves that the synonymy networks of the same language share specific similar structures that can be detected with the help of confluence measures.

5 Conclusion

Although graphs that encode synonymy judgements of standard semantic lexical resources share similar HSW properties they diverge on their synonymy judgements as measured by a low Kappa of edges. So, one could wonder whether the notion of synonymy is well defined, or if synonymy judgements are really independent. Without directly addressing this question, we nevertheless have shown that strong confluence measures help two synonymy graphs accommodate each others' conflicting edges. They reach a much better agreement, whereas random graphs' divergence is maintained. Since the graphs are HSW, they draw clusters of synonyms in which pairs of vertices have a strong confluence.

This suggests two conclusions. First, different synonymy resources that describe the same lexicon reveal dense zones that are much more similar across graphs than the binary synonymy categorisation (the synonym/not synonym alternative). These dense zones convey information about the semantic organisation of the lexicon. Second, random walks and confluence measures seem an appropriate technique to detect and compare the dense zones of various synonymy graphs.

This theoretical work validates the random walk/confluence approach as a potentially valid tool for detecting semantic similarities. This opens many perspectives for applications. For example, it can be used to enrich resources as was done for the Wisigoth project (Sajous et al., 2010). It may also help to merge, or aggregate, resources. If we apply the conciliation process to two graphs G_1 and G_2, obtaining two accommodating graphs $G_1^{(+G_2)} = (V', E_1^+))$ and $G_2^{(+G_1)} = (V', E_2^+))$ then the graph $G = (V', E'' = (E_1^+ \cap E_2^+))$ could be a merged resource. Indeed, G's set of edges, E'' seems like a good compromise because, according to the property 1, $(E_1' \cap E_2') \subseteq E'' \subseteq (E_1' \cup E_2')$. This new aggregation method would need to be validated by comparing the quality of the merged resource to the results of the union or intersection.

Furthermore, this work is a first step for defining a similarity measure between graphs, that could take into account the structural agreement rather than a simple edge-to-edge disagreement. Subsequent work should generalise the conciliation process along several axes:

- The number of steps t was chosen as the shortest possible for the confluence measures. It would be worthwhile to investigate the effect of the length of the walks on the agreement of the accommodating graphs.

- Another line of research would be to alter the conciliation ability of graphs, by increasing or decreasing the criterion for strong confluence. One can for example introduce a k parameter in the definition of C_1 (resp. C_2), in Equation 6:

$$P^t_{G_1'}(u \rightsquigarrow r) > k.\pi_{G_1'}(r) \quad (9)$$

- The conciliation process seems unbalanced insofar as graphs only accept to *add* edges. It should be extended to a negotiating process where a graph could also accept to remove one edge if the other does not have it and its confluence is weak.

- The conciliation process could also be generalised to graphs that have different vertices, such as two synonymy networks of different languages. In that case the issue is not anymore to reveal a deeper similarity, beyond a local disagreement, because one can not compare the graphs vertex by vertex or edge by edge. However, questioning whether the semantic structures revealed by dense zones are similar from one lexicon to another is an interesting line of research. One approach to compare two synonymy graphs of two different languages would be to draw edges between vertices that are translations of each other. Random walks could then reach vertices of the two lexicons, so that the conciliation process could be generalised to accommodating two synonymy graphs via translation links.

Acknowledgements

The research presented in this paper was supported by the ANR-NSC (France-Taiwan) bilateral project M3 (Modeling and Measurement of Meaning). We would like to thank the reviewers for their insightful comments.

References

[Albert and Barabasi2002] Réka Albert and Albert-László Barabasi. 2002. Statistical Mechanics of Complex Networks. *Reviews of Modern Physics*, 74:74–47.

[Bollobas2002] Bela Bollobas. 2002. *Modern Graph Theory*. Springer-Verlag New York Inc., October.

[Cohen1960] Jacob Cohen. 1960. A coefficient of agreement for nominal scales. *Educ. Psychol. Meas.*, (20):27–46.

[Edmonds and Hirst2002] Philip Edmonds and Graeme Hirst. 2002. Near-Synonymy and Lexical Choice. *Computational Linguistics*, 28(2):105–144.

[Fellbaum1998] Christiane Fellbaum, editor. 1998. *WordNet: An Electronic Lexical Database*. MIT Press.

[Gaume et al.2010] Bruno Gaume, Fabien Mathieu, and Emmanuel Navarro. 2010. Building Real-World Complex Networks by Wandering on Random Graphs. *I3: Information Interaction Intelligence*, 10(1).

[Gaume2004] Bruno Gaume. 2004. Balades Aléatoires dans les Petits Mondes Lexicaux. *I3: Information Interaction Intelligence*, 4(2).

[Murray and Green2004] G. Craig Murray and Rebecca Green. 2004. Lexical Knowledge and Human Disagreement on a WSD Task. *Computer Speech & Language*, 18(3):209–222.

[Newman2003] M. E. J. Newman. 2003. The Structure and Function of Complex Networks. *SIAM Review*, 45:167–256.

[Sajous et al.2010] Franck Sajous, Emmanuel Navarro, Bruno Gaume, Laurent Prévot, and Yannick Chudy. 2010. Semi-automatic endogenous enrichment of collaboratively constructed lexical resources: Piggybacking onto wiktionary. In Hrafn Loftsson, Eiríkur Rögnvaldsson, and Sigrún Helgadóttir, editors, *Advances in NLP*, volume 6233 of *LNCS*, pages 332–344. Springer Berlin / Heidelberg.

[Stewart1994] G. W. Stewart. 1994. Perron-frobenius theory: a new proof of the basics. Technical report, College Park, MD, USA.

[Steyvers and Tenenbaum2005] Mark Steyvers and Joshua B. Tenenbaum. 2005. The large-scale structure of semantic networks: Statistical analyses and a model of semantic growth. *Cognitive Science*, 29(1):41–78.

[Watts and Strogatz1998] Duncan J. Watts and Steven H. Strogatz. 1998. Collective Dynamics of Small-World Networks. *Nature*, 393:440–442.

[Zesch et al.2008] Torsten Zesch, Christof Müller, and Iryna Gurevych. 2008. Using wiktionary for computing semantic relatedness. In *Proceedings of the 23rd national conference on Artificial intelligence - Volume 2*, pages 861–866, Chicago, Illinois. AAAI Press.

Word Sense Induction by Community Detection

David Jurgens[1,2]
[1]HRL Laboratories, LLC [2]Department of Computer Science
Malibu, California, USA University of California, Los Angeles
jurgens@cs.ucla.edu

Abstract

Word Sense Induction (WSI) is an unsupervised approach for learning the multiple senses of a word. Graph-based approaches to WSI frequently represent word co-occurrence as a graph and use the statistical properties of the graph to identify the senses. We reinterpret graph-based WSI as community detection, a well studied problem in network science. The relations in the co-occurrence graph give rise to word communities, which distinguish senses. Our results show competitive performance on the SemEval-2010 WSI Task.

1 Introduction

Many words have several distinct meanings. For example, "law" may refer to legislation, a rule, or police depending on the context. Word Sense Induction (WSI) discovers the different senses of a word, such as "law," by examining its contextual uses. By deriving the senses of a word directly from a corpus, WSI is able to identify specialized, topical meanings in domains such as medicine or law, which predefined sense inventories may not include.

aWe consider graph-based approaches to WSI, which typically construct a graph from word occurrences or collocations. The core problem is how to identify sense-specific information within the graph in order to perform sense induction. Current approaches have used clustering (Dorow and Widdows, 2003; Klapaftis and Manandhar, 2008) or statistical graph models (Klapaftis and Manandhar, 2010) to identify sense-specific subgraphs.

We reinterpret the challenge of identifying sense-specific information in a co-occurrence graph as one of *community detection*, where a community is defined as a group of connected nodes that are more connected to each other than to the rest of the graph (Fortunato, 2010). Within the co-occurrence graph, we hypothesize that communities identify sense-specific contexts for each of the terms. Community detection identifies groups of contextual cues that constrain each of the words in a community to a single sense.

To test our hypothesis, we require a community detection algorithm with two key properties: (1) a word may belong to multiple, overlapping communities, which is necessary for discovering multiple senses, and (2) the community detection may be hierarchically tuned, which corresponds to sense granularity. Therefore, we adapt a recent, state of the art approach, Link Clustering (Ahn et al., 2010). Our initial study suggests that community detection offers competitive performance and sense quality.

2 Word Sense Induction

A co-occurrence graph is fundamental to our approach; terms are represented as nodes and an edge between two nodes indicates the terms' co-occurrence, with a weight proportional to frequency. While prior work has focused on clustering the nodes to induce senses, using Link Clustering (Ahn et al., 2010), we cluster the *edges*, which is equivalent to grouping the word collocations to identify sense-specific contexts. We summarize our approach as four steps: (1) selecting the contextual cues, (2) building a co-occurrence graph, (3) performing community detection on the graph, and (4) sense labeling new contexts using the discovered communities.

Context Refinement Representing the co-occurrence graph for all terms in a context is prohibitively expensive. Moreover, often only a subset of the terms in a context constrain the sense of an ambiguous word. Therefore, we refine a word's context to include only a subset of the terms present. Following previous work (Véronis, 2004), we select only nouns in the context.

Early experiments indicated that including infrequent terms in the co-occurrence graph yielded poor performance, which we attribute to having too few connecting edges to identify meaningful community structure. Therefore, we include only those nouns occurring in the most frequent 5000 tokens, which are likely to be representative the largest communities in which a term takes part. Last, we include all the nouns and verbs used in the SemEval 2010 WSI Task (Manandhar et al., 2010), which are used in our evaluation. The selected context terms are then stemmed using the Porter stemmer.

Building the Co-occurrence Graph The graph is iteratively constructed by adding edges between the terms from a context. For each pair-wise combination of terms, an edge is added and its weight is increased by 1. This step effectively embeds a clique if it did not exist before, connecting all of the context's words within the graph. Once all contexts have been seen, the graph is then pruned to remove all edges with weight below a threshold $\tau = 25$. This step removes edges form infrequent collocations, which may not contribute sufficient graph structure for community detection, and as a practical consideration, greatly speeds up the community detection process. However, we note that parameter was largely unoptimized and future work may see a benefit from accounting for edge weight.

Community Detection Within the co-occurrence graph, communities may have partial overlap. For example, Figure 1 illustrates a part of the local graph for "mouse." Two clear senses emerge from the neighbors: one for the input device and another for the animal. However, the terms that correspond to one sense also co-occur with terms corresponding to the other sense, e.g., "information," which hinders finding communities directly from disconnected components in the local neighborhood. Finding sense-specific communities requires recognizing that the co-occurring terms may be shared by multiple communities. Therefore, to identify communi-

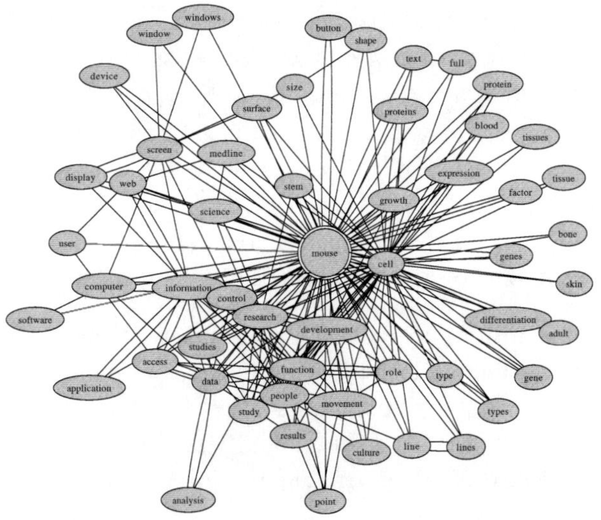

Figure 1: A portion of the local co-occurrence graph for "mouse" from the SemEval-2010 Task 14 corpus

ties we selected the approach of Ahn et al. (2010), summarized next, which performs well for overlapping community structure.

First, the edges are clustered using an unweighted similarity function based on the neighbors of two edges, $e_{i,j}$ and $e_{i,k}$: $sim(e_{i,j}, e_{i,k}) = \frac{n_j \cap n_k}{n_j \cup n_k}$, where n_i denotes the node i and its neighbors. This similarity reflects the percentage of terms that co-occur in common with the term for nodes j and k, independent of the terms that co-occur with the shared term for i. For example, in Figure 1, the similarity for the edges connecting "mouse" with "user" and "software," $\frac{2}{5}$, measures the overlap in the neighbors of "user" and "software" independent of the neighbors for "mouse," such as "cell" and "size."

Using this similarity function, the edges are agglomeratively clustered into a dendrogram. We use the single-link criteria which iteratively merges the two clusters connected by the edge pair with the highest similarity. The dendrogram may then be cut at different levels to reveal different cluster granularities; cuts near the bottom of the dendrogram create a larger number of small groups of collocations, whereas cuts near the top create fewer, larger groups of collocations. To select the specific partitioning of the dendrogram into clusters, we select the solution that maximizes the partition density, which Ahn et al. (2010) define as $D = \frac{2}{M} \sum_c m_c \frac{m_c - (n_c - 1)}{(n_c - 2)(n_c - 1)}$, where M is the number of edges in the graph, c denotes a specific cluster, and n_c and m_c are the number of nodes and edges in cluster c, respectively.

The final set of communities is derived from these partitions: a node is a member of each community in which one of its edges occurs. Last, we remove all communities of size 3 and below, which we interpret as having too few semantic constraints to reliably disambiguate each of its terms.

Sense Induction from Communities Each term in a community is treated as having a specific sense, with one sense per community. To label a contextual usage, we identify the community that best maps to the context. For a given context, made of the set of words W, we score each community i, consisting of words C, using the Jaccard index weighted by community size: $score(C_i, W) = |C_i| \cdot \frac{|C_i \cap W|}{|C_i \cup W|}$. This similarity function favors mapping contexts to larger communities, which we interpret as having more semantic constraints. The final sense labeling consists of the scores for all overlapping communities.

3 Evaluation

We use the SemEval-2 Task 14 evaluation (Manandhar et al., 2010) to measure the quality of induced senses. We summarize the evaluation as follows. Systems are provided with an unlabeled training corpus consisting of 879,807 multi-sentence contexts for 100 polysemous words, comprised of 50 nouns and 50 verbs. Systems induce sense representations for target words from the training corpus and then use those representations to label the senses of the target words in unseen contexts from a test corpus. We use the entire multi-sentence context for building the co-occurrence graph.

The induced sense labeling is scored using two unsupervised and one supervised methods. The unsupervised scores consists of two contrasting measures: the paired FScore (Artiles et al., 2009) and the V-Measure (Rosenberg and Hirschberg, 2007). Briefly, the V-Measure rates the homogeneity and completeness of a clustering solution. Solutions that have word clusters formed from one gold-standard sense are homogeneous; completeness measures the degree to which a gold-standard sense's instances are assigned to a single cluster. The paired FScore reflects the overlap of the solution and the gold standard in cluster assignments for all pair-wise combination of instances. The supervised evaluation transforms the induced sense clusters of a portion of the corpus into a word sense classifier, which is then tested on the remaining corpus. An 80/20 train-test split, $S_{80/20}$, and 60/40 split, $S_{60/40}$, are both used.

	FScore	V-Meas.	$S_{80/20}$	$S_{60/40}$
S_{PD}	61.1 (3)	3.6 (18)	57.64 (18)	57.64 (16)
S_V	56.16 (9)	8.7 (6)	57.90 (18)	57.36 (17)
S_F	63.4 (1)	0 (26)	56.18 (21)	56.20 (21)
Best_F	63.3 (1)	0 (26)	58.69 (14)	58.24 (13)
Best_V	26.7 (25)	16.2 (1)	58.34 (16)	57.27 (17)
Best_S	49.8 (15)	15.7 (2)	62.44 (1)	61.96 (1)
MFS	63.4	0	58.67	58.95

Table 1: Performance results on the SemEval-2010 WSI Task, with rank shown in parentheses. Reference scores of the best submitted systems are shown in the bottom.

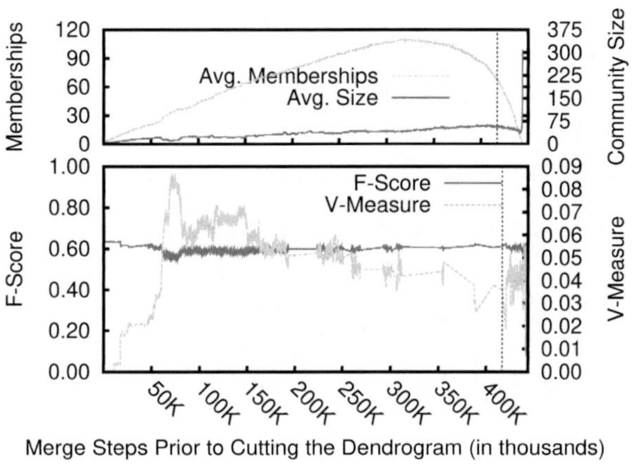

Figure 2: V-Measure and paired FScore results for different partitionings of the dendrogram. The dashed vertical line indicates S_{PD}

Results As a first measure of the quality of the induced senses, we evaluated both the solution that maximized the partition density, referred to as S_{PD}, and an additional 5,000 solutions, evenly distributed among the possible dendrogram partitionings. Figure 2 shows the score distribution for V-Measure and paired FScore. Table 1 lists the scores and rank for S_{PD} and the solutions that optimize the V-Measure, S_V, and FScore, S_F, among the 26 participating Task-14 systems. For comparison, we include the highest performing systems on each measure and the Most Frequent Sense (MFS) baseline.

Discussion Optimizing the partition density results in high performance only for the FScore; however, optimizing for the V-Measure yields competitive performance on both measures. The behavior is encouraging as most approaches submitted to Task 14 favor only one measure.

Figure 2 indicates a relationship between the V-Measure and community memberships. Therefore, using S_V, we calculated the Pearson correlation between a term's scores and the number of community memberships within a single solution. The correlation with the paired FScore, r = -0.167, was not statistically significant at $p < .05$, while correlation with the V-Measure, r = 0.417 is significant with $p <$ 1.6e-5. This suggests that at a specific community granularity, additional communities enable the WSI mapping process to make better sense distinctions between contexts. However, we note that V-Measure begins to drop as the average community membership increases in solutions after S_V, as shown in Figure 2. We suspect that as the agglomerative merge process continues, communities representing different senses become merged, leading to a loss of purity.

The lower performance of S_{PD} and the impact of community memberships raises the important question of how to best select the communities. While co-occurrence graphs have been shown to exhibit small world network patterns (Véronis, 2004), optimizing for the general criterion of partition density that has performed well on such networks does not result in communities that map well to sense-specific contexts. We believe that this behavior is due to impact of the sense inventory; selecting a community solution purely based on the graph's structure may not capture the correct sense distinctions, either having communities with too few members to distinguish between senses or too many members, which conflates senses. However, a promising future direction is to examine whether the there exist features of the graph structure that would allow for recognizing the specific community solutions that correspond directly to different sense granularities without the need for an external evaluation metric.

4 Related Work

We highlight those related works with connections to community detection. Véronis (2004) demonstrated that word co-occurrence graphs follow a small-world network pattern. In his scheme, word senses are discovered by iteratively deleting the more connected portions of the subgraph to reveal the different senses' network structure. Our work capitalizes on this intuition of discovering sense-related subgraphs, but leverages formalized methods for community detection to identify them.

Dorow and Widdows (2003) identify sense-related subgraphs in a similar method to community detection for local region of the co-occurrence graph. They use a random walk approach to identify regions of the graph that are sense-specific. Though not identical, we note that the random walk model has been successfully applied to community detection (Rosvall et al., 2009). Furthermore, Dorow and Widdows (2003) performs graph clustering on a per-word basis; in contrast, the proposed approach identifies communities for the entire graph, effectively performing an all-word WSI.

Klapaftis and Manandhar (2010) capture hierarchical relations between collocations using a Hierarchical Random Graph model where nodes are collocations and edges indicate their co-occurrence, which improved performance over non-hierarchical models. Our community detection approach also captures the hierarchical structure of the collocation graph, but uses a much simpler graphical representation that for n terms requires $O(n)$ nodes and $O(n^2)$ edges, compared to $O(n^2)$ nodes and $O(n^3)$ edges for the above approach, which allows it to build the collocation graph from a larger set of terms.

5 Conclusion

We have proposed a new graph-based method for WSI based on finding sense-specific word communities within a co-occurrence graph, which are then identify distinguish senses in new contexts. An initial analysis using the SemEval-2010 WSI task demonstrates competitive performance. Future research will address two potential avenues: (1) the impact of word frequency on community size and memberships and (2) identifying both graph properties and semantic relations within hierarchical communities that distinguish between sense granularities. Software for the WSI model and for Link Clustering is available as a part of the S-Space Package (Jurgens and Stevens, 2010).

References

Yong-Yeol Ahn, James P. Bagrow, and Sune Lehmann. 2010. Link communities reveal multiscale complexity in networks. *Nature*, (466):761–764, August.

Javier Artiles, Enrique Amigó, and Julio Gonzalo. 2009. The role of named entities in web people search. In *Proceedings of EMNLP*, pages 534–542. ACL.

Beate Dorow and Dominic Widdows. 2003. Discovering corpus-specific word senses. In *Proceedings of the 10th EACL*, pages 79–82.

Santo Fortunato. 2010. Community detection in graphs. *Physics Reports*, 486(3-5):75–174.

David Jurgens and Keith Stevens. 2010. The S-Space Package: An Open Source Package for Word Space Models. In *Proceedings of the ACL 2010 System Demonstrations*.

Ioannis P. Klapaftis and Suresh Manandhar. 2008. Word sense induction using graphs of collocations. In *Proceeding of ECAI 2008*, pages 298–302.

Ioannis P. Klapaftis and Suresh Manandhar. 2010. Word sense induction & disambiguation using hierarchical random graphs. In *Proceedings of EMNLP*, pages 745–755. ACL.

Suresh Manandhar, Ioannis P. Klapaftis, Dmitriy Dligach, and Sameer S. Pradhan. 2010. SemEval-2010 task 14: Word sense induction & disambiguation. In *Proceedings of the 5th International Workshop on Semantic Evaluation*, pages 63–68. Association for Computational Linguistics.

Andrew Rosenberg and Julia Hirschberg. 2007. V-measure: A conditional entropy-based external cluster evaluation measure. In *Proceedings of the Joint Conference of EMNLP-CoNLL*. ACL, June.

M. Rosvall, D. Axelsson, and C.T. Bergstrom. 2009. The map equation. *The European Physical Journal-Special Topics*, 178(1):13–23.

J. Véronis. 2004. HyperLex: lexical cartography for information retrieval. *Computer Speech & Language*, 18(3):223–252.

Using a Wikipedia-based Semantic Relatedness Measure for Document Clustering

Majid Yazdani
Idiap Research Institute and EPFL
Centre du Parc, Rue Marconi 19
1920 Martigny, Switzerland
majid.yazdani@idiap.ch

Andrei Popescu-Belis
Idiap Research Institute
Centre du Parc, Rue Marconi 19
1920 Martigny, Switzerland
andrei.popescu-belis@idiap.ch

Abstract

A graph-based distance between Wikipedia articles is defined using a random walk model, which estimates visiting probability (VP) between articles using two types of links: hyperlinks and lexical similarity relations. The VP to and from a set of articles is then computed, and approximations are proposed to make tractable the computation of semantic relatedness between every two texts in a large data set. The model is applied to document clustering on the 20 Newsgroups data set. Precision and recall are improved in comparison with previous textual distance algorithms.

1 Introduction

Many approaches have been proposed to compute similarity between texts, from lexical overlap measures to statistical topic models that are learned from large corpora. In this paper, we propose a method for using knowledge from a structured, collaborative resource – the Wikipedia hypertext encyclopedia – in order to build a measure of semantic relatedness that we test on a text clustering task.

The paper first describes the document graph derived from Wikipedia (Section 2), and then defines a network-based distance using visiting probability (Section 3), along with algorithms for its application to text clustering (Section 4). Results over the 20 Newsgroups dataset are shown to be competitive (Section 5), and the relative contributions of cosine lexical similarity and visiting probability are analyzed. Our proposal is discussed in the light of previous work in Section 6.

2 The Document Network

In the present proposal, knowledge about semantic relatedness is embodied into a document network, whose nodes are intended to represent concepts, while the links between nodes stand for various relations between concepts. The nodes of the network correspond to articles from the Wikipedia hypertext encyclopedia, and are derived as follows.

The network was built from Wikipedia, using the WEX dataset (Metaweb Technologies, 2010). All articles from the following categories were removed, as they do not correspond to proper concepts: Talk, File, Image, Template, Category, Portal, and List. Moreover, disambiguation pages and articles shorter than 100 non-stopwords were filtered out as well. Out of 4,327,482 articles in WEX, 1,264,611 articles were kept, forming the nodes of our network.

The first type of links in our document network are the hyperlinks between articles, because, in principle, each link between two articles indicates some form of relatedness between them. There are more than 35 million such links in our network.

The second type of links is derived from the similarity of lexical content between articles. This is computed using cosine similarity between the lexical vectors corresponding to the articles' texts, after stopword removal and stemming. Then, links are created by connecting every article to the 10 articles that are most similar to it, each link receiving a weight which is the normalized lexical similarity score. The number 10 was chosen to ensure computational tractability, and is in the same range as the average number of hyperlinks per node (30).

Computing semantic relatedness between two texts requires: (1) to estimate relatedness between two sets of nodes in the network, as described in Sections 3 and 4; and (2) to project each text onto a set of nodes, as we briefly explain here. The projection of a text onto the network is found by computing the text's lexical similarity with all articles, again using cosine distance over stemmed words, without stopwords. The text is mapped to the 10 closest articles, resulting in a probability distribution over the 10 corresponding nodes. Again, this value was chosen to be similar to the number of hyperlinks and content links per node, and to keep computation tractable. In fact, the numerous Wikipedia articles are scattered in the space of words, therefore tuning these values does not seem to bring crucial changes.

3 Computing Relatedness in the Network Using Visiting Probability (VP)

We have previously defined a random walk model (Yazdani and Popescu-Belis, 2010) to compute relatedness of sets of nodes as the visiting probability (VP) of a random walker from one set to another one, and we will review the model in this section. In the next section, we will explain how the model was extended for application to document clustering.

3.1 Notations

Let $S = \{s_i | 1 \leq i \leq n\}$ be the set of n nodes in the graph. Any two nodes s_i and s_j can be connected by one or more directed and weighted links, which can be of L different types ($L = 2$ in our case: hyperlinks and lexical similarity links). Links between nodes can thus be represented by L matrices A_l ($1 \leq l \leq L$) of size $n \times n$, where $A_l(i, j)$ is the weight of the link of type l between s_i and s_j. The *transition matrix* C_l gives the probability of a direct transition between nodes s_i and s_j, using only links of type l. This matrix can be built from the A_l matrix as follows:

$$C_l(i, j) = \frac{A_l(i, j)}{\sum_{k=1}^{n} A_l(i, k)}.$$

In the random walk process using all link types ($1 \leq l \leq L$), let the weight w_l denote the importance of link type l. Then, the overall transition matrix C giving the transition probability $C_{i,j}$ between nodes s_i and s_j is : $C = \sum_{l=1}^{L} w_l C_l$.

One of the main parameters in this computation is the relative weight of the two types of links (lexical similarity and hyperlinks) in the random walk over the network. The settings for the experiments on document clustering (0.6 vs. 0.4) are explained in Section 5.1 below.

3.2 VP from a Set of Nodes to a Node

Let us consider a probability distribution $\vec{r}$ over nodes, corresponding to the projection of a text fragment onto the network of articles (Section 2). Given a new node s_j in the network, our model first estimates the probability of visiting s_j for the first time when a random walker starts from $\vec{r}$ in the graph. The model considers the state S_t of the random walker (its position node) and provides a procedure which, executed until termination, yields the value of VP. Namely, the initial state is chosen at random with probability $P(S_0 = s_i | \vec{r}) = r_i$ (where the r_i are the components of $\vec{r}$). Then, from state S_{t-1}, either $S_{t-1} = s_j$ and the procedure is finished, or the next node is chosen using the transition matrix C. Moreover, it is also possible to 'fail' the walk with a small probability, called 'absorption probability', which makes longer paths less probable.

3.3 Differences between VP and PageRank or Hitting Time

The VP of s_j starting from the distribution $\vec{r}$, as computed here, is different from the probability assigned to s_j after running Personalized PageRank (Haveliwala, 2003) with a teleport vector equal to $\vec{r}$. In the computation of VP, the loops starting from s_j and ending to the same s_j do not have any effect on the final score, unlike for PPR, for which such loops boost the probability of s_j. If some pages have this type of loops (typically, very "popular" pages), then after using PPR they will have high probability although they might not be very close to the teleport vector $\vec{r}$.

The VP of s_j is also different from the hitting time to s_j, defined as the average number of steps a random walker would take to visit s_j for the first time in the graph starting from $\vec{r}$. Hitting time is more sensitive to long paths in comparison to VP, a fact that might introduce more noise.The performance of these three algorithms in computing semantic similarity has been compared in (Yazdani and Popescu-Belis, 2010).

3.4 VP between Sets of Nodes

Generalizing now to the computation of VP from a weighted set of nodes $\vec{r}_1$ (a probability distribution) to another set $\vec{r}_2$, the model first constructs a virtual node representing $\vec{r}_2$ in the network, named by convention s_R, and then connects all nodes s_i to s_R according to their weights in $\vec{r}_2$. The transition matrix for the random walk is updated accordingly.

To compute relatedness of two texts projected onto the network as $\vec{r}_1$ and $\vec{r}_2$, the VP of $\vec{r}_1$ given $\vec{r}_2$ is averaged with the converse probability, of $\vec{r}_2$ given $\vec{r}_1$ – a larger probability indicating closer semantic relatedness.

3.5 Truncated VP

The computation of VP can be done iteratively and can be truncated after a number of steps, as the importance of longer paths grows smaller due to the absorption probability, leading thus to a T-truncated visiting probability noted VP^T. Besides making computation more tractable, truncation reduces the effect of longer paths, which seem to be less reliable indicators of relatedness.

We have computed an upper bound on the truncation error, which helps to control and minimize the number of steps actually computed in a random walk. To compute the upper bound of the truncation error we compute the probability of returning neither success (reaching s_j) nor failure (absorption) in first t steps, which can be computed as $\sum_{i\neq j}^{n} \alpha^t(\vec{r}C'^t)_i$. This is in fact the probability mass at time t at all nodes except s_j, the targeted node. C' is the transition matrix that gives the probability of a transition between two nodes, modified to include the virtual node s_R in the network, and $1-\alpha$ is the absorption probability.

If $p_t(success)$ denotes the probability of success (reaching s_j) considering paths of length at most t, and ε_t the error made by truncating after step t, then we have:

$$\varepsilon_t = p(success) - p_t(success) \leq \sum_{i\neq j}^{n} \alpha^t(\vec{r}C'^t)_i$$

So, if $p_t(success)$ is used as an approximation for $p(success)$ then an upper bound for this approximation error ε_t is the right term of the above inequality.

4 Application of VP to Text Clustering

In this section, we describe the additional modeling that was done so that semantic relatedness based on VP could be applied efficiently to text clustering. Indeed, it is not tractable to individually compute the average VP between any two texts in the set of documents to be clustered, because the numbers of pairs is very large – e.g., 20,000 documents in the experiments in Section 5. Instead, we propose two solutions for computing, respectively, *VP to* a set of nodes (from all documents in the network), and respectively *VP from* a set of nodes to all documents.

4.1 Computing VP from All Nodes to a Subset

To compute the T-truncated visiting probability (noted VP^T) from all nodes in the network to a node s_R at the same time, the following recursive procedure is defined. Here, T is the number of steps before truncation, and s_R is a virtual node representing a probability distribution $\vec{r}$ from a text. The procedure is based on the definition of VP between nodes in Section 3 and uses the transition matrix C' that gives the probability of a transition between two nodes, modified to include the virtual node s_R in the network. If $1-\alpha$ is the absorption probability, then the recursive definition of VP^T from a node s_i to the virtual node s_R is:

$$VP^T(s_i, s_R) = \alpha \sum_k C'(s_i, s_k) VP^{T-1}(s_k, s_R)$$

Using dynamic programming, it is possible to compute VP^T from all nodes to s_R in $O(ET)$ steps, where E is the number of links in the network. The initialization of the procedure is done using $VP^T(s_R, s_R) = 1$ and $VP^0(s_i, s_R) = 0$ for any $i \neq R$.

4.2 Computing VP from a Subset to All Nodes

To compute the truncated *VP from* $\vec{r}$ to all nodes in the network, the total computation time using the definition of VP^T from Section 3 is $O(ETN)$, where N is the number of nodes in the network, because VP^T must be computed for each node separately. For a large data set, this is not tractable.

The proposed solution is based on a sampling method over the random walks to approximate VP^T. The sampling involves running M independent random walks of length T from $\vec{r}$. For a given node s_j and a sample walk m, the first time (if any) when s_j is visited on each random walk starting from $\vec{r}$ is noted t_{jm}. Then, VP^T can be estimated by the following average over sample walks, where $1 - \alpha$ is again the absorption probability:

$$\hat{VP^T}(\vec{r}, s_j) = (\sum_m \alpha^{t_{jm}})/M.$$

As a result, the estimate of VP^T can be computed in $O(MT)$ steps, where M is the number of sample paths.

Moreover, it is possible to compute a bound on the error of the estimation, $|\, VP^T - \hat{VP^T}\,|$, depending on the number of sample paths M. It can be shown that the error is lower than ε, with a probability larger than $1 - \delta$, on condition that the number of sample paths is greater than $\alpha^2 \ln(2/\delta)/2\varepsilon^2$.

To prove this bound, we use inspiration from a proof by Sarkar et al. (2008). If the estimation of a variable X is noted $\hat{X}$, let us suppose that concept s_j has been visited for the first time at $\{t_{j_1}, \cdots, t_{j_m}\}$ time steps in the M sample walks. We define the random variable X^l by $\alpha^{t_{j_l}}/M$, where t_{j_l} indicates the time step at which s_j was visited for the first time in l^{th} sampling. If s_j was not visited at all, then $X^l = 0$ by convention. The l random variables X^l $(j_1 \leq l \leq j_m)$ are independent and bounded by 0 and 1 $(0 \leq X^l \leq 1)$. We have:

$$\hat{VP^T}(\vec{r}, s_j) = \sum_l X^l = (\sum_l \alpha^{t_{j_l}})/M \text{ and}$$

$$E(\hat{VP^T}(\vec{r}, s_j)) = VP^T(\vec{r}, s_j).$$

So, by applying Hoeffding's inequality, we have:

$$P(|\hat{VP^T} - E(\hat{VP^T})| \geq \epsilon) \leq 2exp(-\frac{2M\epsilon^2}{\alpha^2}).$$

If the probability of error must be at most δ, then setting the right side lower than δ gives the bound for M that is stated in our theorem.

As a consequence, we have the following lower bound for M if we want ε-approximation for all possible s_j with probability at least $1 - \delta$. We use union bound and Hoeffding's inequality:

$$P(\exists j \in \{1, \ldots, n\}, |\hat{VP^T} - E(\hat{VP^T})| \geq \epsilon) \leq 2n \times exp(-\frac{2M\epsilon^2}{\alpha^2})$$

which gives the lower bound $M \geq \frac{\alpha^2 \ln(2n/\delta)}{2\epsilon^2}$.

5 Document Clustering

This section describes the experimental setting and the results of applying the text relatedness measure defined above to the problem of document clustering over the 20 Newsgroups dataset.[1] The dataset contains about 20,000 postings to 20 news groups, hence 20 document classes, with about 1,000 documents per class. We aim here at finding these classes automatically, using for testing the entire data set without using any part of it as a training set. The knowledge of our system comes entirely from the document network and the techniques for computing distances between two texts projected onto it.

5.1 Setup of the Experiment

We first compute a similarity matrix for the entire 20 Newsgroups data set, with the relatedness score between any two documents being VP^T. For tractability, we fixed $T = 5$ that gives sufficient precision; a larger value only increased computation time. Instead of computing VP^T between all possible pairs separately, we fill one row of the matrix at a time using the approximations above.

We set the absorption probability of the random walk $1 - \alpha = 0.2$ for this experiment. Given α and T by using the formula in section 3.5, it is possible to compute the error bound of the truncation, and noting that for a smaller α, fewer steps (T) are needed to achieve the same approximation precision because of the penalty set to longer paths. Conversely, a larger α decreases the penalty for longer paths and requires more computation.[2]

For comparison purposes, four similarity matrices were computed. Indeed, the theoretical apparatus described above can be applied to various types of links in the document network. In Section 2, we introduced two types of links, namely lexical similarity and actual hyperlinks, and these can be used separately in the model, or as a weighted combination. The following similarities will be compared:

1. VP over hyperlinks only (noted VP_{Hyp});
2. VP over lexical similarity links (VP_{Lex});

[1]Distributed at `http://www.cs.cmu.edu/afs/cs.cmu.edu/project/theo-20/www/data/news20.html`, see also (Mitchell, 1997, Chapter 6).

[2]Note that in the extreme case when $\alpha = 0$, similarity to all nodes except the node itself is zero.

3. VP over a combination of hyperlinks (0.4) and lexical links (0.6) (noted VP_{Comb}) – these values gave the best results in our previous applications to word and document similarity tasks (Yazdani and Popescu-Belis, 2010);

4. no random walk, only cosine similarity between the tf-idf vectors of the documents to be clustered (noted LS, for lexical similarity).

5.2 Clustering Performance

Clustering is performed using a k-means algorithm over each of the four similarity matrices.[3] The quality of the clustering is first measured using the Rand Index (RI), which counts the proportion of pairs of documents that are similarly grouped, i.e. either in the same, or in different clusters, in the reference vs. candidate clusterings. Other methods exist (Pantel and Lin, 2002), including a Rand Index adjusted for chance (Vinh et al., 2009), but the RI suffices for comparative judgments in this subsection. However, in Subsection 5.3, we will also look at precision and recall, and in Subsection 5.4 we will use purity. As the clustering is performed over the entire data set, because there is no training vs. test data, confidence intervals are not available, though they could be computed by splitting the data. As a result, comparison with other scores on the same test set is absolute.

The scores in terms of Rand Index are, in decreasing order:

1. 90.8% for VP_{Comb}
2. 90.6% for VP_{Hyp}
3. 90.4% for VP_{Lex}
4. and only 86.1% for the LS cosine similarity.

The random walk model thus clearly outperforms the baseline LS approach. If counting only wrongly clustered document pairs, VP_{Comb} has 6.6% of such pairs, while VP_{Lex} has 8.4%, confirming the lower performance of the model using only lexical similarity links, i.e. the utility of hyperlinks.

[3]The semantic relatedness measure proposed here could be used with other clustering algorithms, such as the committee-based method proposed by Pantel and Lin (2002).

5.3 Comparison to Other Methods

To obtain a better understanding of the performance of the proposed method, we computed the clustering precision and recall of several well-known methods for statistical text representation, shown in Table 1. For Latent Dirichlet Allocation (LDA) (Blei et al., 2003) and Latent Semantic Analysis (LSA) (Deerwester et al., 1990), we first mapped the documents in the latent space and then computed the cosine similarity between the documents in the latent space. The number of topics for LSA and LDA is set to 100 to make the computation tractable. Precision and recall are used, rather than the Rand Index, to show in more detail the performance of each method. The use of VP over our document network clearly increases both precision and recall in comparison to other tested approaches.

Similarity method	Precision	Recall
LS	7.50	18.38
LSA	8.63	9.99
LDA	19.93	31.50
VP_{Comb}	**23.81**	**35.32**

Table 1: Precision and Recall for k-means clustering over the 20 Newsgroups using several well-known methods to compute text similarity, in comparison to the present proposal.

5.4 Analysis of the Impact of VP with Respect to Cosine Similarity

To find out in which cases the proposed method improves over a simple cosine similarity measure, we considered a linear combination of the cosine similarity and VP, noted $w \times VP_{Comb} + (1 - w) \times LS$, and varied the weight w from 0 to 1. Considering the k-nearest neighbors of every document according to this combined similarity, we define k-purity as the number of documents with the correct label over the total number of documents k in the computed neighborhood. The variation of k-purity with w, for several values of k, is shown in Figure 1.

The best purity appears to be obtained for a combination of the two methods, for all values of k that were tested. This shows that VP_{Comb} brings valuable additional information about document relatedness that cannot be found in LS only. Further-

Figure 1: Values of k-purity (vertical axis) averaged over all documents, for neighborhoods of different sizes k. The horizontal axis indicates the weight w of visiting probability vs. cosine lexical similarity in the formula: $w \times VP_{Comb} + (1 - w) \times LS$.

more, when the size of the examined neighborhood k increases (lower curves in Figure 1), the effect of VP_{Comb} becomes more important, i.e. its weight in the optimal combination increases. For very small neighborhoods, LS is almost sufficient to ensure optimal purity, but for larger ones ($k = 10$ or 15), VP_{Comb} used alone ($w = 1$) outperforms LS used alone ($w = 0$). Their optimal combination leads to scores that are higher than those obtained for each of them used separately, and, as noted, the weight of VP_{Comb} in the optimal combination increases for larger neighborhoods.

These results can be explained as follows. For very small neighborhoods, the cosine lexical similarity score with the nearest 1–5 documents is very high, as they have many words in common, so LS is a good measure of text relatedness. However, when looking at larger neighborhoods, for which relatedness is less based on identical words, then VP_{Comb} becomes more effective, and LS performs poorly. Therefore, we can predict that VP_{Comb} will be most relevant when looking for larger neighborhoods, or in order to increase recall. VP_{Comb} should also be relevant when there is low diversity among document words, for instance when all documents are very short.

6 Related Work

Many attempts have been made to improve the overlap-based lexical similarity distance, for various applications to HLT. One approach is to construct a taxonomy of concepts and relations (manually or automatically) and to map the text fragments to be compared onto the taxonomy. For instance, Wordnet (Fellbaum, 1998) and Cyc (Lenat, 1995) are two well-known knowledge bases that can be used for enriching pure lexical matching. However, building and maintaining such resources requires considerable effort, and they might cover only a fraction of the vocabulary of a language, as they usually include few proper names or technical terminology.

Another approach makes use of unsupervised methods to construct a semantic representation of documents by analyzing mainly co-occurrence relationships between words in a corpus. Latent Semantic Analysis (Deerwester et al., 1990), Probabilistic LSA (Hofmann, 1999) and Latent Dirichlet Allocation (Blei et al., 2003) are unsupervised methods that construct a low-dimensional feature representation or concept space, in which words are no longer supposed to be independent.

Mihalcea et al. (2006) compared knowledge-based and corpus-based methods, using word similarity and word specificity to define one general measure of text semantic similarity. Because it computes word similarity values between all word pairs, the proposed method appears to be suitable mainly to compute similarity between short fragments, otherwise the computation becomes intractable.

WikiRelate! (Strube and Ponzetto, 2006) computes semantic relatedness between two words by using Wikipedia. Each word is mapped to the corresponding Wikipedia article by using article titles. To compute relatedness, several methods are proposed, namely, using paths in the Wikipedia category structure or the articles' content. Our method, by comparison, also uses the knowledge embedded in the hyperlinks between articles, as well as the entire contents of articles, but unlike WikiRelate! it has been extended to texts of arbitrary lengths.

Explicit Semantic Analysis (Gabrilovich and Markovitch, 2007), instead of mapping a text to a node or a small group of nodes in a taxonomy, maps the text to the entire collection of available concepts, by computing the degree of affinity of each concept to the input text. Similarity is measured in the new concept space. ESA does not use the link structure or other structured knowledge from Wikipedia. Moreover, by walking over a content similarity graph, our method benefits from a nonlinear distance measure according to the paths consisting of small neighborhoods.

In the work of Yeh et al. (2009), a graph of documents and hyperlinks is computed from Wikipedia, then a Personalized PageRank (Haveliwala, 2003) is computed for each text fragment, with the teleport vector being the one resulting from the ESA algorithm cited above. To compute semantic relatedness between two texts, Yeh et al. (2009) simply compare their personalized page rank vectors. By comparison, in our method, we also consider in addition to hyperlinks the effect of word co-occurrence between article contents. The use of visiting probability also gives different results over personalized page rank, as it measures different properties of the network.

There are many studies on measuring distances between vertices in a graph. Two measures that are close to the visiting probability proposed here are hitting time and Personalized PageRank mentioned in Section 3.3. Hitting time has been used in various studies as a distance measure in graphs, e.g. for dimensionality reduction (Saerens et al., 2004) or for collaborative filtering in a recommender system (Brand, 2005). Hitting time was also used for link prediction in social networks along with other distances (Liben-Nowell and Kleinberg, 2003), or for semantic query suggestion using a query/URL bipartite graph (Mei et al., 2008). As for Personalized PageRank, it was used for word sense disambiguation (Agirre and Soroa, 2009), and for measuring lexical relatedness of words in a graph built from WordNet (Hughes and Ramage, 2007).

7 Conclusion

We proposed a model for measuring text semantic relatedness based on knowledge embodied in Wikipedia, seen here as document network with two types of links – hyperlinks and lexical similarity ones. We have used visiting probability to measure proximity between weighted sets of nodes, and have proposed approximation algorithms to make computation efficient for large graphs (more than one million nodes and 40 million links) and large text clustering datasets (20,000 documents in 20 Newsgroups). Results on the document clustering task showed an improvement using both word co-occurrence information and user-defined hyperlinks between articles over other methods for text representation.

Acknowledgments

The work presented in this paper has been supported by the IM2 NCCR (Interactive Multimodal Information Management) of the Swiss National Science Foundation (http://www.im2.ch).

References

Eneko Agirre and Aitor Soroa. 2009. Personalizing pagerank for word sense disambiguation. In *Proceedings of EACL 2009 (12th Conference of the European Chapter of the Association for Computational Linguistics)*, pages 33–41, Athens, Greece.

David M. Blei, Andrew Y. Ng, and Michael I. Jordan. 2003. Latent Dirichlet Allocation. *Journal of Machine Learning Research*, 3:993–1022.

Matthew Brand. 2005. A random walks perspective on maximizing satisfaction and profit. In *Proceedings of the 2005 SIAM International Conference on Data Mining*, Newport Beach, CA.

Scott Deerwester, Susan T. Dumais, George W. Furnas, Thomas K. Landauer, and Richard Harshman. 1990. Indexing by Latent Semantic Analysis. *Journal of the American Society for Information Science*, 41(6):391–407.

Christiane Fellbaum, editor. 1998. *WordNet: An electronic lexical database*. MIT Press, Cambridge, MA.

Evgeniy Gabrilovich and Shaul Markovitch. 2007. Computing semantic relatedness using Wikipedia-based explicit semantic analysis. In *Proceedings of IJCAI 2007 (20th International Joint Conference on Artificial Intelligence)*, pages 6–12, Hyderabad.

Taher H. Haveliwala. 2003. Topic-sensitive pagerank: A context-sensitive ranking algorithm for web search. *IEEE Transactions on Knowledge and Data Engineering*, 15:784–796.

Thomas Hofmann. 1999. Probabilistic Latent Semantic Indexing. In *Proceedings of SIGIR 1999 (22nd ACM SIGIR Conference on Research and Development in Information Retrieval)*, pages 50–57, Berkeley, CA.

Thad Hughes and Daniel Ramage. 2007. Lexical semantic relatedness with random graph walks. In *Proceedings of EMNLP-CoNLL 2007 (Conference on Empirical Methods in Natural Language Processing and Conference on Computational Natural Language Learning)*, pages 581–589, Prague.

Douglas B. Lenat. 1995. CYC: A large-scale investment in knowledge infrastructure. *Communications of the ACM*, 38(11):33–38.

David Liben-Nowell and Jon Kleinberg. 2003. The link prediction problem for social networks. In *Proceedings of CIKM 2003 (12th ACM International Conference on Information and Knowledge Management)*, pages 556–559, New Orleans, LA.

Qiaozhu Mei, Dengyong Zhou, and Kenneth Church. 2008. Query suggestion using hitting time. In *Proceeding of CIKM 2008 (17th ACM International Conference on Information and Knowledge Management)*, pages 469–478, Napa Valley, CA.

Metaweb Technologies. 2010. Freebase Wikipedia Extraction (WEX). http://download.freebase.com/wex/.

Rada Mihalcea, Courtney Corley, and Carlo Strapparava. 2006. Corpus-based and knowledge-based measures of text semantic similarity. In *Proceedings of AAAI 2006 (21st National Conference on Artificial Intelligence)*, pages 775–782, Boston, MA.

Tom M. Mitchell. 1997. *Machine Learning*. McGraw-Hill, New York.

Patrick Pantel and Dekang Lin. 2002. Document clustering with committees. In *Proceedings of SIGIR 2002 (25th Annual International ACM SIGIR Conference on Research and Development in Information Retrieval)*, pages 199–206, Tampere.

Marco Saerens, Franois Fouss, Luh Yen, and Pierre Dupont. 2004. The principal components analysis of a graph, and its relationships to spectral clustering. In *Proceedings of ECML 2004 (15th European Conference on Machine Learning)*, pages 371–383, Pisa.

Purnamrita Sarkar, Andrew W. Moore, and Amit Prakash. 2008. Fast incremental proximity search in large graphs. In *Proceedings of ICML 2008 (25th International Conference on Machine Learning)*, pages 896–903, Helsinki.

Michael Strube and Simone Paolo Ponzetto. 2006. Wikirelate! Computing semantic relatedness using Wikipedia. In *Proceedings of AAAI 2006 (21st National Conference on Artificial Intelligence)*, pages 1419–1424.

Nguyen Xuan Vinh, Julien Epps, and James Bailey. 2009. Information theoretic measures for clusterings comparison: Is a correction for chance necessary? In *Proceedings of ICML 2009 (26th International Conference on Machine Learning)*, Montreal.

Majid Yazdani and Andrei Popescu-Belis. 2010. A random walk framework to compute textual semantic similarity: a unified model for three benchmark tasks. In *Proceedings of IEEE ICSC 2010 (4th IEEE International Conference on Semantic Computing)*, Pittsburgh, PA.

Eric Yeh, Daniel Ramage, Christopher D. Manning, Eneko Agirre, and Aitor Soroa. 2009. WikiWalk: random walks on Wikipedia for semantic relatedness. In *Proceedings of TextGraphs-4 (4th Workshop on Graph-based Methods for Natural Language Processing)*, pages 41–49, Singapore.

GrawlTCQ: Terminology and Corpora Building by Ranking Simultaneously Terms, Queries and Documents using Graph Random Walks

Clément de Groc
Syllabs
Univ. Paris Sud
LIMSI-CNRS
cdegroc@limsi.fr

Xavier Tannier
Univ. Paris Sud
LIMSI-CNRS
xtannier@limsi.fr

Javier Couto
Syllabs
MoDyCo (UMR 7114, CNRS-UPX)
jcouto@syllabs.com

Abstract

In this paper, we present GrawlTCQ, a new bootstrapping algorithm for building specialized terminology, corpora and queries, based on a graph model. We model links between documents, terms and queries, and use a random walk with restart algorithm to compute relevance propagation. We have evaluated GrawlTCQ on an AFP English corpus of 57,441 news over 10 categories. For corpora building, GrawlTCQ outperforms the BootCaT tool, which is vastly used in the domain. For 1,000 documents retrieved, we improve mean precision by 25%. GrawlTCQ has also shown to be faster and more robust than BootCaT over iterations.

1 Introduction

Specialized terminology and corpora are key resources in applications such as machine translation or lexicon-based classification, but they are expensive to develop because of the manual validation required. Bootstrapping is a powerful technique for minimizing the cost of building these resources.

In this paper, we present GrawlTCQ[1], a bootstrapping algorithm for building specialized terminology, corpora and queries: from a small set of user-provided terms, GrawlTCQ builds the resources via automated queries to a search engine. The algorithm relies on a graph that encodes the three kinds of entities involved in the procedure (*terms*, *documents* and *queries*) and relations between them. We model the relevance propagation in our graph by using a random walk with restart algorithm.

We use BootCaT (Baroni and Bernardini, 2004) as our baseline because it is a similar algorithm that has been vastly used and validated experimentally in the domain. We have evaluated GrawlTCQ and BootCaT on an AFP (Agence France Presse) English corpus of 57,441 news over 10 categories. Results show that, for corpora building, GrawlTCQ significantly outperforms the BootCaT algorithm. As this is an on-going work, further work is needed to evaluate terminology and query results.

The article is structured as follows: in Section 2, we review the related work in terminology and corpora construction using bootstrapping techniques, as well as random walk applications. In Section 3, we describe GrawlTCQ. In Section 4, we evaluate GrawlTCQ and compare its results with those provided by BootCaT. We conclude in Section 5.

2 Related Work

Several works using bootstrapping techniques have been carried out in terminology and corpora creation. For example, (Ghani et al., 2005) has built minority language corpora from the web. The Web-as-Corpus WaCky initiative (Baroni et al., 2009; Ferraresi et al., 2008; Sharoff, 2006) has built very large web-derived corpus in various languages. They used previously mentioned BootCaT tool to do this. As the quality of the results is strongly dependent on the quality of seed terms and the underlying search engine, manual filtering is usually mandatory to enhance performance. GrawlTCQ uses a graph to automatically filter out erroneous terms and documents

[1] GrawlTCQ stands for Graph RAndom WaLk for Terminology, Corpora and Queries.

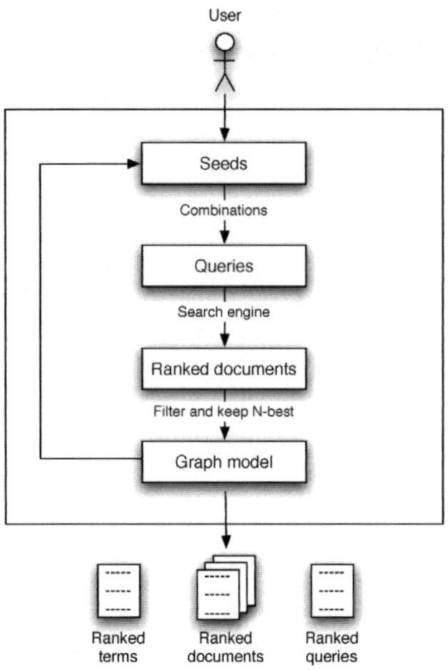

Figure 1: Components of the GrawlTCQ algorithm.

and improve the system's overall performance. The manual filtering cost is therefore drastically reduced.

Graph modeling and random walks have been applied with success to many different domains of NLP, such as keyword and sentence extraction (Mihalcea and Tarau, 2004), computer-science articles ranking (Nie et al., 2005), web pages ranking (Haveliwala, 2002; Page et al., 1999; Richardson and Domingos, 2002), WordNet-based word sense disambiguation (Agirre and Soroa, 2009) and lexical semantic relatedness (Hughes and Ramage, 2007), or set expansion (Wang and Cohen, 2007). In this paper, we confirm the relevance of this approach to terminology and corpora bootstrapping.

3 Ranking simultaneously Terms, Queries and Documents

3.1 The GrawlTCQ bootstrapping algorithm

Figure 1 shows the components of the GrawlTCQ algorithm. Starting from user provided seed terms[2], GrawlTCQ iteratively creates queries, finds documents and extracts new terms. We model this bootstrapping procedure with a graph that keeps all links between documents, terms and queries. Our hypothesis is that the information added will increase the procedure's robustness and overall performances. The graph model (see figure 2) is built online. As common terms will occur in many documents and thus have high centrality, they will end with high scores. In order to avoid this effect, document-term edges are weighted with a TermHood measure (Kageura and Umino, 1996) such as tfidf or log odds ratio.

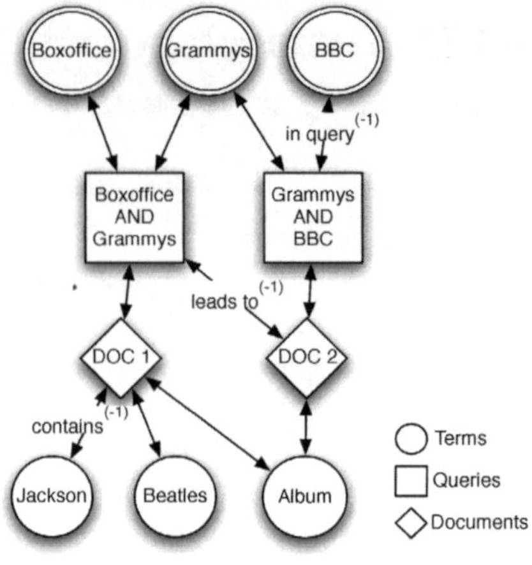

Figure 2: Sample subgraph using "boxoffice", "Grammys" and "BBC" as seed terms.

By using a random walk with restart algorithm, also known as personalized PageRank (Haveliwala, 2002), terms, queries and documents are weighted globally and simultaneously. At the end of each iteration of GrawlTCQ, a random walk is computed and the resulting stationary distribution is used to rank documents and terms[3]. If more documents are needed, then the algorithm executes one more step.

Several parameters can be specified by the user, such as the number of seed terms, the number of terms composing a query, as well as the number of documents retrieved for each query. In addition, the algorithm may use the Internet (with search engines as Google, Yahoo! or Bing), an Intranet, or both, as data sources. When using the web as source, specific algorithms must be used to remove HTML boilerplate (Finn et al., 2001) and filter un-useful documents (duplicates (Broder, 2000), webspam and error pages (Fletcher, 2004)).

[2]These terms may be easily computed from a list of seed urls or documents, using terminology extraction techniques.

[3]As an additional result, we also obtain a ranked list of queries.

3.2 Graph Walk

Considering a directed graph $G = (V, E)$, the score of a vertex V_i is defined as

$$PR(V_i) = (1 - \alpha)\lambda_0 + \alpha \times \sum_{j \in In(V_i)} \frac{PR(V_j)}{|Out(V_j)|}$$

where $In(V_i)$ (resp. $Out(V_i)$) are V_i predecessors (resp. successors). In the original PageRank algorithm, a damping factor α of 0.85 has been used and the personalization vector (or teleportation vector) λ_0 is distributed uniformly over V. On the contrary, (Richardson and Domingos, 2002) and (Haveliwala, 2002) have proposed to personalize the PageRank according to a user query or a chosen topic. Following previous work (Page et al., 1999; Mihalcea and Tarau, 2004), we have fixed the damping factor to 0.85[4] and the convergence threshold to 10^{-8}.

As we have different types of edges carrying different relations, we slightly modify the PageRank formula, as in (Wang and Cohen, 2007): when walking away from a node, the random surfer first picks randomly a relation type and then chooses uniformly between all edges of the chosen relation type. Biasing the algorithm to insist more on seed terms is a legitimate lead as these nodes represent the strong base of our model. We thus use a custom λ_0 distribution that spreads weights uniformly over the seed terms instead of the whole set of vertices.

4 Evaluation

Evaluating the proposed method on the web can hardly be done without laborious manual annotation. Moreover, web-based evaluations are not reproducible as search engines index and ranking functions change over time. This is especially a problem when evaluating the impact of different parameters of our algorithm. In this article, we have chosen to carry out an objective and reproducible evaluation based on a stable and annotated document collection.

The AFP has provided us an English corpus composed of 57,441 news documents written between January 1st and March 31, 2010. We have considered the 17 top-level categories from the IPTC standard (http://www.iptc.org). Documents are categorized in one or more of those categories and are annotated with various metadata, such as keywords. As some categories contained too few documents, we have only kept the 10 largest ones (see table 1). The corpus was then indexed using Apache Lucene (http://lucene.apache.org) in order to create a basic search engine[5]. This setup has several advantages: first, the document collection is stable and quantifiable. Documents are clean text written in a journalistic style. As they are already annotated, several automatic evaluations can be run with different parameters. Finally, querying the search engine and retrieving documents can be done efficiently. However, note that, as the document collection is limited, queries might return few or no results (which is rarely the case on the web).

Id	Category	#docs
01	Arts, culture and entertainment	3074
02	Crime, law and justice	5675
03	Disaster and accident	4602
04	Economy, business and finance	13321
08	Human interest	1300
11	Politics	17848
12	Religion and belief	1491
14	Social issue	1764
15	Sport	15089
16	Unrest, conflicts and war	8589

Table 1: AFP corpus categories distribution.

We have used the BootCaT algorithm as our baseline. To the best of our knowledge this is the first attempt to rigorously evaluate BootCaT performances. We have compared both algorithms in exactly the same conditions, on a task-based experiment: to retrieve 50, 100, 300, 500 and 1000 documents for each category, independently of the number of iterations done.

To be as close as possible to the original BootCaT algorithm, we have weighted document-term edges by log odds ratio. This measure allows us to distinguish common terms by using a reference background corpus. In all our experiments, we have used the ukWac corpus (Ferraresi et al., 2008), a very large web-derived corpus, for this purpose.

In order to select initial seed terms we have used documents' metadata. We have computed the fre-

[4] During our experiments, we haven't observed any significant change when modifying this parameter.

[5] All normalization features except lower-casing were disabled to allow ease of reproducibility.

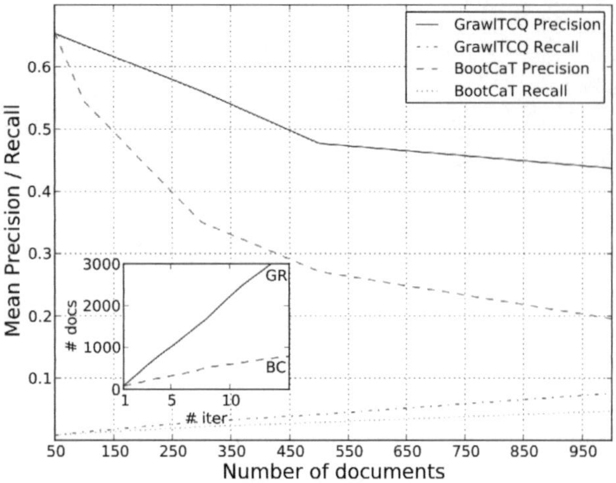

Figure 3: Mean precision and recall at 50, 100, 300, 500 and 1000 documents (inset: Mean number of documents / number of iterations)

quency of occurrences of a keyword in a category and have then divided this score by the sum of occurrences in all other categories. This strategy leads to relevant seed terms that are not necessarily exclusive to a category. For instance, selected seeds for the 4th category are: *economics*, *summary*, *rate*, *opec*, *distress*, *recession*, *zain*, *jal*, *gold*, and *spyker*.

We have fixed a number of parameters for our experiments: at each iteration, the top-10 seeds are selected (either from the initial set or from newly extracted terms). Queries are composed of 2 seeds, all 45 possible combinations[6] are used and a total of 10 documents are retrieved for each query.

All scores are averaged over the 10 categories. As can be seen in figure 3, GrawlTCQ shows much more robustness and outperforms BootCaT by 25% precision at 1000 documents. Detailed results for each category are shown in table 2 and confirm the relevance of our approach. Interestingly, BootCaT and GrawlTCQ have very low precisions for the 14th category (*Social issue*). Documents found in this category are often ambiguous and both algorithms fail to extract the domain terminology. We have also plotted the number of documents in function of the number of iterations as shown in figure 3 (inset). The curve clearly shows that GrawlTCQ yields more

[6]When running the same experiment with randomly selected tuples several times, we have found similar results when averaging all runs output.

CatId	P@50		P@100		P@300		P@500		P@1000	
	GR	BC	GR	BC	GR	BC	GR	BC	GR	BC
01	**0.58**	0.50	**0.57**	0.30	**0.43**	0.12	**0.35**	0.08	**0.23**	0.05
02	0.44	**0.60**	**0.45**	0.33	**0.46**	0.17	**0.44**	0.10	**0.34**	0.07
03	0.82	0.82	**0.99**	0.81	**0.89**	0.41	**0.66**	0.26	**0.54**	0.14
04	**0.86**	0.80	0.82	**0.85**	**0.84**	0.55	**0.78**	0.34	**0.79**	0.19
08	**0.79**	0.79	0.44	**0.48**	0.23	**0.42**	0.17	**0.40**	0.20	**0.39**
11	0.76	**0.78**	0.79	**0.81**	**0.87**	0.71	0.57	**0.64**	**0.57**	0.56
12	0.46	**0.54**	**0.35**	0.27	**0.20**	0.10	**0.17**	0.06	**0.15**	0.03
14	0.08	**0.24**	**0.13**	0.10	**0.06**	0.04	**0.04**	0.02	**0.04**	0.02
15	1.0	1.0	1.0	1.0	**0.92**	0.78	**0.87**	0.67	**0.81**	0.39
16	**0.82**	0.56	**0.81**	0.49	**0.71**	0.21	**0.72**	0.15	**0.70**	0.13

Table 2: Precision at various cutoffs by category

documents at a faster rate. This is due to the seed selection process: GrawlTCQ's queries lead to many documents while BootCaT queries often lead to few or no documents. Moreover, as we can see in figure 3, while fetching more documents faster, the mean precision of GrawlTCQ is still higher than the BootCaT one which shows that selected seeds are, at the same time, more prolific and more relevant.

5 Conclusion

In this paper, we have tackled the problem of terminology and corpora bootstrapping. We have proposed GrawlTCQ, an algorithm that relies on a graph model including terms, queries, and documents to track each entity origin. We have used a random walk algorithm over our graph in order to globally and simultaneously compute a ranking for each entity type. We have evaluated GrawlTCQ on a large news dataset and have shown interesting gain over the BootCaT baseline. We have especially obtained better results without any human intervention, reducing radically the cost of manual filtering. We are considering several leads for future work. First, we must evaluate GrawlTCQ for query and term ranking. Then, while preliminary experiments have shown very promising results on the web, we would like to setup a large scale rigorous evaluation. Finally, we will conduct further experiments on edges weighting and seed terms selection strategies.

Acknowledgments

We would like to thank the AFP for providing us the annotated news corpus. This work was partially funded by the ANR research project ANR-08-CORD-013.

References

Eneko Agirre and Aitor Soroa. 2009. Personalizing PageRank for word sense disambiguation. In *Proceedings of the 12th Conference of the European Chapter of the Association for Computational Linguistics on - EACL, 2009*.

Marco Baroni and Silvia Bernardini. 2004. BootCaT: Bootstrapping Corpora and Terms from the Web. In *Proceedings of the LREC 2004 conference*.

Marco Baroni, Silvia Bernardini, Adriano Ferraresi, and Eros Zanchetta. 2009. The WaCky Wide Web : A Collection of Very Large Linguistically Processed Web-Crawled Corpora. In *Proceedings of the LREC 2009 conference*, volume 43, pages 209–226.

Andrei Z Broder. 2000. Identifying and Filtering Near-Duplicate Documents. In *Proceedings of the 11th Annual Symposium on Combinatorial Pattern Matching*, pages 1–10, London, UK. Springer-Verlag.

Adriano Ferraresi, Eros Zanchetta, Marco Baroni, and Silvia Bernardini. 2008. Introducing and evaluating ukwac, a very large web-derived corpus of english. In *Proceedings of the 4th Web as Corpus Workshop (WAC-4)*, pages 47–54.

Aidan Finn, Nicholas Kushmerick, and Barry Smyth. 2001. Fact or fiction: Content classification for digital libraries. In *DELOS Workshop: Personalisation and Recommender Systems in Digital Libraries*.

William H Fletcher. 2004. Making the Web More Useful as a Source for Linguistic Corpora. *Corpus Linguistics in North America*, (January 2003):191–205.

Rayid Ghani, Rosie Jones, and Dunja Mladenic. 2005. Building Minority Language Corpora by Learning to Generate Web Search Queries. *Knowl. Inf. Syst.*, 7(1):56–83.

Taher H. Haveliwala. 2002. Topic-sensitive PageRank. *Proceedings of the eleventh international conference on World Wide Web - WWW '02*, page 517.

Thad Hughes and Daniel Ramage. 2007. Lexical Semantic Relatedness with Random Graph Walks. In *Proceedings of EMNLP, 2007*, pages 581–589.

Kyo Kageura and Bin Umino. 1996. Methods of automatic term recognition: A review. *Terminology*, 3(2):259–289.

Rada Mihalcea and Paul Tarau. 2004. TextRank bringing order into text. In *Proceedings of EMNLP*, pages 404–411. Barcelona: ACL.

Zaiqing Nie, Yuanzhi Zhang, J.R. Wen, and W.Y. Ma. 2005. Object-level ranking: Bringing order to web objects. In *Proceedings of the 14th international conference on World Wide Web*, pages 567–574. ACM.

Lawrence Page, Sergey Brin, Rajeev Motwani, and Terry Winograd. 1999. The PageRank Citation Ranking: Bringing Order to the Web. Technical report, Stanford InfoLab.

M. Richardson and P. Domingos. 2002. The intelligent surfer: Probabilistic combination of link and content information in pagerank. *Advances in Neural Information Processing Systems*, 2:1441–1448.

Serge Sharoff. 2006. Creating general-purpose corpora using automated search engine queries. *M. Baroni, S. Bernardini (eds.) WaCky! Working papers on the Web as Corpus, Bologna, 2006*, pages 63–98.

Richard C. Wang and William W. Cohen. 2007. Language-independent set expansion of named entities using the web. *Proceedings of IEEE International Conference on Data Mining (ICDM 2007), Omaha, NE, USA. 2007.*

Simultaneous Similarity Learning and Feature-Weight Learning for Document Clustering

Pradeep Muthukrishnan
Dept of CSE,
University of Michigan
mpradeep@umich.edu

Dragomir Radev
School of Information,
Dept of CSE,
University of Michigan
radev@umich.edu

Qiaozhu Mei
School of Information,
Dept of CSE,
University of Michigan
qmei@umich.edu

Abstract

A key problem in document classification and clustering is learning the similarity between documents. Traditional approaches include estimating similarity between feature vectors of documents where the vectors are computed using TF-IDF in the bag-of-words model. However, these approaches do not work well when either similar documents do not use the same vocabulary or the feature vectors are not estimated correctly.

In this paper, we represent documents and keywords using multiple layers of connected graphs. We pose the problem of *simultaneously* learning similarity between documents and keyword weights as an edge-weight regularization problem over the different layers of graphs. Unlike most feature weight learning algorithms, we propose an unsupervised algorithm in the proposed framework to simultaneously optimize similarity and the keyword weights. We extrinsically evaluate the performance of the proposed similarity measure on two different tasks, clustering and classification. The proposed similarity measure outperforms the similarity measure proposed by (Muthukrishnan et al., 2010), a state-of-the-art classification algorithm (Zhou and Burges, 2007) and three different baselines on a variety of standard, large data sets.

1 Introduction

The recent upsurge in the amount of text available due to the widespread growth of the Internet has led to the need for large scale, efficient Machine Learning (ML), Information Retrieval (IR) tools for text mining. At the heart of many of the ML, IR algorithms is the need for a good similarity measure between documents. For example, a better similarity measure almost always leads to better performance in tasks like document classification, clustering, etc.

Traditional approaches represent documents with many keywords using a simple feature vector description. Then, similarity between two documents is estimated using the dot product between their corresponding vectors. However, such similarity measures do not use all the keywords *together* and hence, suffer from problems due to sparsity. There are two major issues in computing similarity between documents

- Similar documents may not use the same vocabulary.
- Estimating feature weights or weight of a keyword to the document it is contained in.

For example, consider two publications, X and Y, in the field of Machine Learning. Let X be a paper on clustering while Y is on classification. Although the two publications use very different vocabulary, they are semantically similar. Keyword weights are mostly estimated using the frequency of the keyword in the document. For example, TF-IDF based scoring is the most commonly used approach to compute keyword weights to compute similarity between documents. However, suppose publications X and Y mention the keyword "'Machine Learning"' only once. Although, they are mentioned only once in the text of the document, for the purposes of computing semantic similarity between the documents, it would be beneficial to give it a high keyword weight.

A commonly used approach to estimate semantic similarity between documents is to use an external knowledge source like WordNet (Pedersen et al., 2004). However, these approaches are domain dependent and language dependent. If document similarity can not be estimated accurately using just the text, there have been approaches incorporating multiple sources of similarity like link similarity, authorship similarity between publications (Bach et al., 2004; Cortes et al., 2009). (Muthukrishnan et al., 2010) also uses multiple sources of similarity. In addition to improving similarity estimates between documents, it also improves similarity estimates between keywords. Co-clustering (Dhillon et al., 2003) based approaches are used to alleviate problems due to the sparsity and high-dimensionality of the data. In co-clustering, the keywords and the documents are *simultaneously* clustered by exploiting the duality between them. However, the approach relies solely on the keyword distributions to cluster the documents and vice-versa. It does not take into account the inherent similarity between the keywords (documents) when clustering the documents (keywords). Also, co-clustering takes as input the weight of all keywords to corresponding documents.

2 Motivation

First, we explain how similarity learning and feature weight learning can mutually benefit from each other using an example. For example, consider the following three publications in the field of Machine Translation, (Brown et al., 1990; Gale and Church, 1991; Marcu and Wong, 2002)

Clearly, all the papers belong to the field of *Machine Translation* but (Gale and Church, 1991) contains the phrase "'Machine Translation"' only once in the entire text. However, we can learn to attribute some similarity between (Brown et al., 1990) and the second publication using the text in (Marcu and Wong, 2002). The keywords "'Bilingual Corpora"' and "'Machine Translation"' co-occur in the text in (Marcu and Wong, 2002) which makes the keywords themselves similar. Now we can attribute some similarity between the (Brown et al., 1990) and (Marcu and Wong, 2002) publication since they contain similar keywords. This shows how similarity learning can benefit from important keywords.

Now, assume that "'Machine Translation"' is an *important* keyword (high keyword weight) for the first and third publication while "'Bilingual Corpora"' is an important keyword for the second publication. We explained how to infer similarity between the first and second publication using the third publication as a bridge. Using the newly learned similarity measure, we can infer that "'Bilingual Corpora"' is an *important* keyword for the second publication since a similar keyword ("'Machine Translation"') is an important keyword for similar publications.

Let documents D_i and D_j contain keywords K_{ik} and K_{jl}. Then intuitively, the similarity between two documents should be jointly proportional to

- The similarity between keywords K_{ik} and K_{jl}
- The weights of K_{ik} to D_i and K_{jl} to D_j.

Similarly the weight of a keyword K_{ik} to document D_i should be jointly proportional to

- The similarity between documents D_i and D_j.
- The similarity between keyphrases K_{ik} and K_{jl} and weight of K_{jl} to D_j.

The major contributions of the paper are given below,

- A rich representation model for representing documents with associated keywords for efficiently estimating document similarity..
- A regularization framework for *joint* feature weight (keyword weight) learning and similarity learning.
- An unsupervised algorithm in the proposed framework to efficiently learn similarity between documents and the weights of keywords for each document in a set of documents.

In the next two sections, we formalize and exploit this observation to jointly optimize similarity between documents and weight of keywords to documents in a principled way.

3 Problem Formulation

We assume that a set of keywords have been extracted for the set of documents to be analyzed. The setup is very general: Documents are represented by the set of candidate keywords. In addition to that, we have crude initial similarities estimated between documents and also between keywords and the weights of keywords to documents. The similarities and keyword weights are represented using two layers of graphs. We formally define the necessary concepts,

Definition 1: Documents and corresponding keywords
We have a set of N documents $D = \{d_1, d_2, \ldots, d_N\}$. Each document, d_i has a set of m_i keywords $K_i = \{k_{i1}, k_{i2}, \ldots, k_{im_i}\}$

Definition 2: Document Similarity Graph
The document similarity graph, $G_1 = (V_1, E_1)$, consists of the set of documents as nodes and the edge weights represent the initial similarity between the documents.

Definition 3: Keyword Similarity Graph
The keyword similarity graph, $G_2 = (V_2, E_2)$, consists of the set of keywords as nodes and the edge weights represent the initial similarity between the keywords.

The document similarity graph and the keyword similarity graph can be considered as two layers of graphs which are connected by the function defined below

Definition 4: keyword Weights (KW)
There exists an edge between d_i and k_{ij} for $1 \leq j \leq m_i$. Let Z represent the keyword weighting function, i.e, $Z_{d_i,k_{ij}}$ represents the weight of keyword k_{ij} t document d_i.

4 Regularization Framework

$$\begin{aligned}\Omega(w, Z) &= \alpha_0 * ISC(w, w*) + \alpha_1 * IKC(Z, Z*) \\ &+ \alpha_2 * KS(w, Z) + \alpha_3 * SK(Z, w) \quad (1)\end{aligned}$$

where $\alpha_0 + \alpha_1 + \alpha_2 + \alpha_3 = 1$.

ISC refers to **I**nitial **S**imilarity **C**riterion and *IKC* refers to **I**nitial **K**eyword weight **C**riterion. They are defined as follows

$$ISC(w, w*) = \sum_{u,v \in G_1} (w_{u,v} - w^*_{u,v})^2 \quad (2)$$

$$IKC(Z, Z*) = \sum_{u \in G_1, v \in G_2} (Z_{u,v} - Z^*_{u,v})^2 \quad (3)$$

KS refers to **K**eyword based **S**imilarity and *SK* refers to **S**imilarity induced **K**eyword weight. They are defined as follows

$$\begin{aligned}KS(w, Z) = &\sum_{u_1,v_1 \in G_1} \sum_{u_2,v_2 \in G_2} Z_{u_1,u_2} Z_{v_1,v_2} \\ &(w_{u_1,v_1} - w_{u_2,v_2})^2 \quad (4)\end{aligned}$$

and

$$\begin{aligned}SK(w, Z) = &\sum_{u_1,v_1 \in G_1} \sum_{u_2,v_2 \in G_2} w_{u_1,v_1} w_{u_2,v_2} \\ &(Z_{u_1,u_2} - Z_{v_1,v_2})^2 \quad (5)\end{aligned}$$

Then the task is to minimize the objective function. The objective function consists of four parts. The first and second parts are initial similarity criterion and initial keyword criterion. They ensure that the optimized edge weights are close to the initial edge weights. The weights α_0 and α_1 ensure that the optimized weights are close to the initial weights, in other words, they represent the confidence level in initial weights.

The significance of the third and the fourth parts of the objective function are best explained by a simple example. Consider two graphs, G_1 and G_2. Let G_1 be the graph containing publications as nodes and edge weights representing initial similarity values. Let G_2 be the graph corresponding to keywords and edge weights represent similarity between keywords. There is an edge from a node u_1 in G_1 to a node v_1 in G_2 if the publication corresponding to u_1 contains the keyword corresponding to v_1.

According to this example, minimizing the keyword weight induced similarity part corresponds to updating similarity values between keywords in proportion to weights of the keywords to the respective documents they are contained in and the similarity between the documents. keyword weight induced similarity part also helps updating similarity values between documents in proportion to weights of keywords they contain and the similarity between the contained keywords.

Minimizing the similarity induced keyword part corresponds to updating keyword weights in proportion to the following

- Similarity between v_1 and other keywords $v_2 \in G_2$
- Keyword weight of v_2 to documents $u_2 \in G_1$
- Similarity between u_1 and u_2

Therefore, even if frequency of a keyword such as "'Machine Translation"' in a publication is not high, it can achieve a high keyword weight if it contains many other similar keywords such as "'Bilingual Corpora"' and "'Word alignment"'.

5 Efficient Algorithm

We seek to minimize the objective function using Alternating Optimization (AO) (Bezdek and Hathaway, 2002), an approximate optimization method. Alternating optimization is an iterative procedure for minimizing (or maximizing) the function $f(x) = f(X_1, X_2, \ldots, X_t)$ jointly over all variables by alternating restricted minimizations over the individual subsets of variables $X_1, \ldots, X_t$.

In this optimization method, we partition the set of variables into a set of mutually exclusive, exhaustive subsets. We iteratively perform minimizations over each subset of variables while maintaining the other subsets of variables fixed. Formally, let the set of real-valued variables be $X = \{X_1, X_2, \ldots, X_N\}$ be partitioned into m subsets, $\{Y_1, Y_2, \ldots, Y_m\}$. Also, let $s_i = |Y_i|$. Then we begin with the initial set of values $\{Y_1^0, Y_2{}^0, \ldots, Y_m{}^0\}$ and make restricted minimizations of the following form,

$$\min_{Y_i \in \mathbb{R}^{s_i}} \{f(\underline{Y_1}^{r+1}, \ldots, \underline{Y_{i-1}}^{r+1}, Y_i, \underline{Y_{i+1}}^{r}, \ldots, \underline{Y_m}^{r})\} \tag{6}$$

where $i = 1, 2, \ldots, m$. The ***underline notation*** $\underline{Y_j}$ indicates that the subset of variables Y_j are fixed with respect to Y_i. In the context of our problem, we update each edge weight while maintaining other edge weights to be a constant. Then the problem boils down to the minimization problem over a single edge weight. For example, let us solve the minimization problem for edge weight corresponding to (u_i, v_j) where $u_i, v_j \in G_1$ (The case where $u_i, v_j \in G_2$ is analogous). Clearly the objective function is a convex function in $w_(u_i, v_j)$. The partial derivative of the objective function with respect to the edge weight is given below,

$$\begin{aligned}\frac{\partial \Omega(w, Z)}{\partial w_{u_i,v_j}} &= 2\alpha_0(w_{u_i,v_j} - w^*_{u_i,v_j}) \\ &+ 2\alpha_2 * \sum_{u_2,v_2 \in G_2} (w_{u_i,v_j} - \underline{w_{u_2,v_2}})\underline{Z_{u_1,u_2}}\underline{Z_{v_j,v_2}} \\ &+ \alpha_3 * \sum_{u_2,v_2 \in G_2} (\underline{Z_{u_i,u_2}} - \underline{Z_{v_j,v_2}})^2 w_{u_i,v_j}\underline{w_{u_2,v_2}}\end{aligned}$$

. (7)

To minimize the above function, we set the partial derivative to zero which gives us the following expression,

$$\begin{aligned}w_{u_j,v_k} = {} & \frac{1}{C_1}(\alpha_0 w^*_{u_i,v_j} + \\ & \alpha_2 \sum_{u_2,v_2 \in G_2} \underline{Z_{u_i,u_2}}\,\underline{w_{u_2,v_2}}\,\underline{Z_{v_j,v_2}}) \end{aligned} \tag{8}$$

where

$$\begin{aligned}C_1 = {} & \alpha_0 + \alpha_2 \sum_{u_2,v_2 \in G_2} \underline{Z_{u_i,u_2}}\,\underline{Z_{v_j,v_2}} \\ & + \frac{\alpha_3}{2} \sum_{u_2,v_2 \in G_2} (\underline{Z_{u_i,u_2}} - \underline{Z_{v_j,v_2}})^2 \underline{w_{u_2,v_2}}\end{aligned}$$

Similarly, we can derive the update equation for keyword weights, Z_{u_i,u_j} as below,

$$\begin{aligned}Z_{u_i,u_j} &= \frac{1}{C_2}(\alpha_1 Z^*_{u_i,u_j} + \\ & \alpha_3 \sum_{v_1 \in G_1} \sum_{v_2 \in G_2} \underline{w_{u_i,v_1}}\,\underline{w_{u_j,v_2}}\,\underline{Z_{v_1,v_2}})\end{aligned} \tag{9}$$

where,

$$\begin{aligned}C_2 = {} & \alpha_1 + \alpha_3 \sum_{v_1 \in G_1} \sum_{v_2 \in G_2} \underline{w_{u_i,v_1}}\,\underline{w_{u_j,v_2}} \\ & + \frac{\alpha_2}{2} \sum_{v_1 \in G_1} \sum_{v_2 \in G_2} (\underline{w_{u_i,v_1}} - \underline{w_{u_j,v_2}})^2 \underline{Z_{v_1,v_2}}\end{aligned}$$

The similarity score between two nodes is proportional to the similarity between nodes in the other layer. For example, the similarity between two documents (keywords) is proportional to the similarity between the keywords the documents they contain (the documents they are contained in). C plays the role of a normalization constant. Therefore, for similarity between two nodes to be high, it is required that they not only contain a lot of similar nodes in the other graph but the similar nodes need to be important to the two target nodes.

Similarly, a particular keyword will have a high weight to a document if similar keywords have high weights to similar documents. Also, it is necessary that the similarity between the keywords and the documents are high.

It can be shown that equations 8 and 9 converge $q-linearly$ since the minimization problem is convex in each of the variables individually and hence has a global and unique minimizer (Bezdek and Hathaway, 2002).

5.1 Layered Random Walk Interpretation

The above algorithm has a very nice intuitive interpreation in terms of random walks over the two different graphs. Assume the initial weights are transition probability values after the graphs are normalized so that each row of the adjacency matrices sums to 1. Then the similarity between two nodes u and v in the same graph is computed as sum of two parts. The first part is α_0 times the initial similarity. This is necessary so that the optimized similarity values are not too far away from the initial similarity values. The second part corresponds to the probability of a random walk of length 3 starting at u and reaching v through two intermediate nodes from the other graph.

The semantics of the random walk depends on whether u, v are documents or keywords. For example, if the two nodes are documents, then the similarity between two documents d_1 and d_2 is the probability of random walk starting at document d_1 and then moving to a keyword k_1 and then moving to keyword k_2 and then to document d_2. Note that keywords k_1 and k_2 can be the same keyword which accounts for similarity between documents because they contain the same keyword.

Also, note that second and higher order dependencies are also taken into account by this algorithm. That is, two papers may become similar because they contain two keywords which are connected by a path in the keyword graph, whose length is greater than 1. This is due to the iterative nature of the algorithm. For example, keywords "'Machine Translation"' and "'Bilingual corpora"' occur often together and hence any co-occurrence based similarity measure will assign a high initial similarity value. Hence two publications which contain these words will be assigned a non-zero similarity value after a single iteration. Also, "'Bilingual corpora"' and "'SMT"' (abbreviation for Statistical Machine Translation) can have a high initial similarity value which enables assiging a high similarity value between "'Machine Translation"' and "'SMT"'. This leads to a chain effect as the number of iterations increases which helps assign non-zero similarity values between semantically similar documents even if they do not contain common keywords.

6 Experiments

It is very hard to evaluate similarity measures in isolation. Thus, most of the algorithms to compute similarity scores are evaluated extrinsically, i.e, the similarity scores are used for an external task like clustering or classification and the performance in the external task is used as the performance measure for the similarity scores. This also helps demonstrate the different applications of the computed similarity measure. Thus, we perform a variety of different experiments on standard data sets to illustrate the improved performance of the proposed similarity measure. There are three natural variants of the algorithm,

- *Unified*: We compare against the edge-weight regularization algorithm proposed in (Muthukrishnan et al., 2010). The algorithm has the same representation as our algorithm but the optimization is strictly defined over the edge weights in the two layers of the graph, $w_ij's$ and not on the keyword weights. Therefore, Z_ij are maintained constant throughout the algorithm.

- *Unified-binary*: In this variant, we initialize the keyword weights to 1, i.e, $Z_ij = 1$ whenever document i contains the keyword j.

ACL-ID	Paper Title	Research Topic
W05-0812	Improved HMM Alignment Models for Languages With Scarce Resources	Machine Translation
P07-1111	A Re-Examination of Machine Learning Approaches for Sentence-Level MT Evaluation	Machine Translation
P03-1054	Accurate Unlexicalized Parsing	Dependency Parsing
P07-1050	K-Best Spanning Tree Parsing	Dependency Parsing
P88-1020	Planning Coherent Multi-Sentential Text	Summarization

Table 1: Details of a few sample papers classified according to research topic

- *Unified-TFIDF*: We initialize the keyword weights to the TFIDF scores, Z_ij is set to the TFIDF score of keyword j for document i.

Experiment Set I: We compare our similarity measure against other similarity measures in the context of classification. We also compare against a state of the art classification algorithm which uses different similarity measures due to different feature types without integrating them into one single similarity measure. Specifically, we compare our algorithm against three other similarity baselines in the context of classification which are listed below.

- *Content Similarity*: Similarity is computed using just the feature vector representation using just the text. We use cosine similarity after preprocessing each document into a tf.idf vector for the AAN data set. For all other data sets, we use the cosine similarity on the binary feature vector representation that is available.

- *Link Similarity*: Similarity is computed using only the links (citations, in the case of publications). To compute link similarity, we use the node similarity algorithm proposed by (Harel and Koren, 2001) using a random walk of length 3 on the link graph.

- *Linear combination*: The content similarity (CS) and link similarity (LS) between documents x and y are combined in a linear fashion as $\alpha CS(x, y) + (1 - \alpha)LS(x, y)$. We tried different values of α and report only the best accuracy that can be achieved using linear combination of similarity measures. Note that this is an upper bound on the accuracy of Multiple Kernel Learning with the restriction of the combination being affine.

We also compare our algorithm against the following algorithms *SC-MV*: We compare our algorithm against the spectral classification algorithm for data with multiple views (Zhou and Burges, 2007). The algorithm tries to classify data when multiple views of the data are available. The multiple views are represented using multiple homogeneous graphs with a common vertex set. In each graph, the edge weights represent similarity between the nodes computed using a single feature type. For our experiments, we used the link similarity graph and the content similarity graph as described above as the two views of the same data

We use a semi-supervised graph classification algorithm (Zhu et al., 2003) to perform the classification.

Experiment Set II: We illustrate the improved performance of our similarity measure in the context of clustering. We compare our similarity measure against the three similarity baselines mentioned above. We use a spectral graph clustering algorithm proposed in (Dhillon et al., 2007) to perform the clustering.

We performed our experiments on three different data sets. The three data sets are explained below.

- AAN Data: The ACL Anthology is a collection of papers from the Computational Linguistics journal as well as proceedings from ACL conferences and workshops and includes 15,160 papers. To build the ACL Anthology Network (AAN), (Radev et al., 2009) manually performed some preprocessing tasks including parsing references and building the network metadata, the citation, and the author collaboration networks. The full AAN includes the raw text of all the papers in addition to full citation and collaboration networks.

  We chose a subset of papers in 3 topics (Ma-

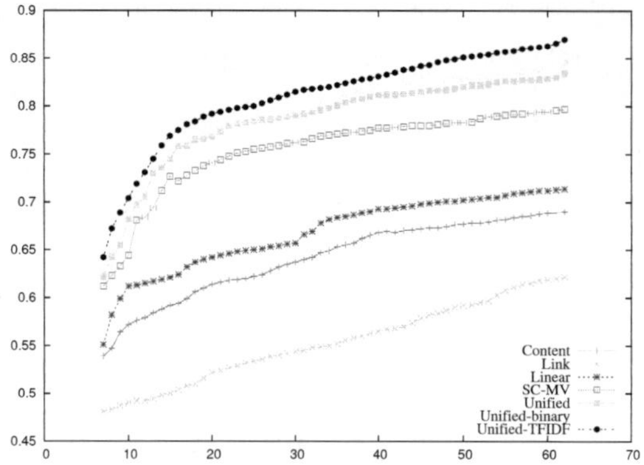

(a) AAN

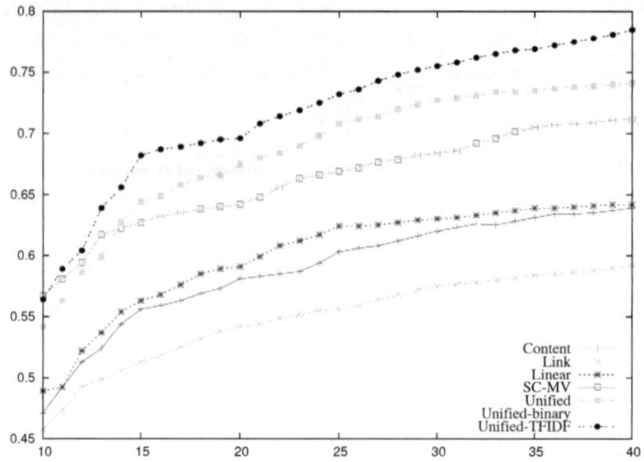

(b) Cornell

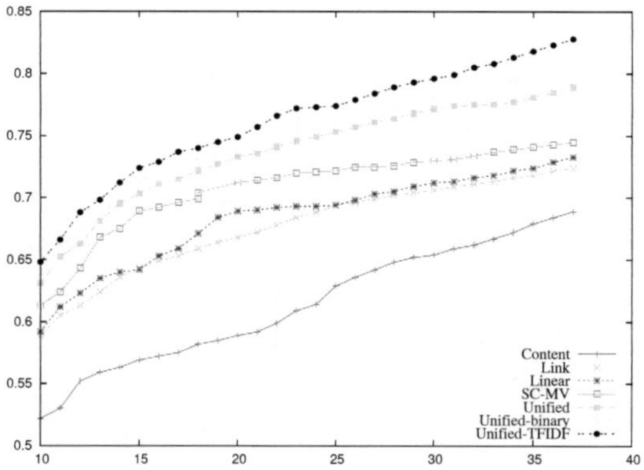

(c) Texas

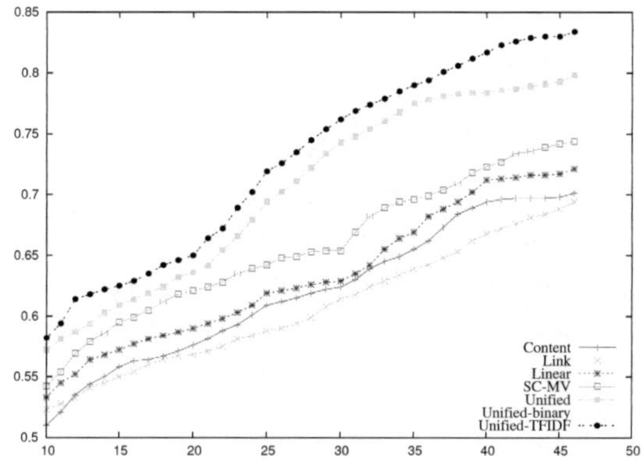

(d) Washington

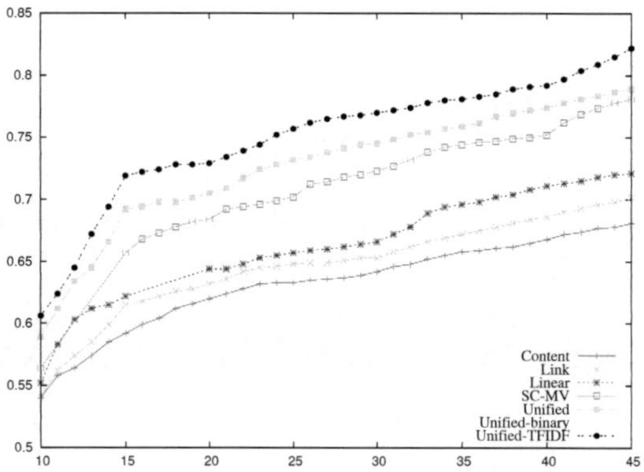

(e) Wisconsin

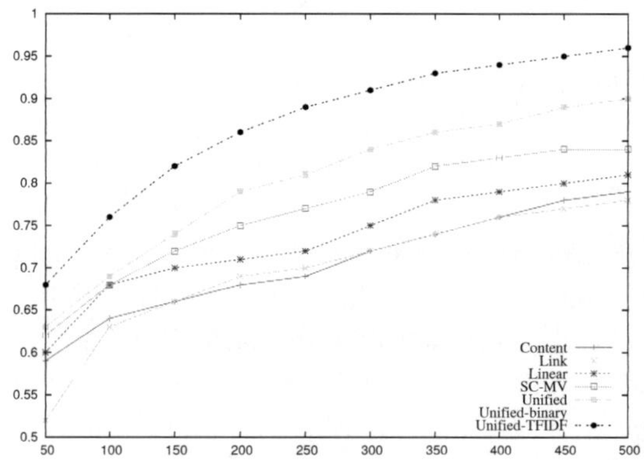

(f) Cora

Figure 1: Classification Accuracy on the different data sets. The number of points labeled is plotted along the x-axis and the y-axis shows the classification accuracy on the unlabeled data.

chine Translation, Dependency Parsing, Summarization) from the ACL anthology. These topics are three main research areas in Natural Language Processing (NLP). Specifically, we collected all papers which were cited by papers whose titles contain any of the following phrases, "'Dependency Parsing"', "'Machine Translation"', "'Summarization"'. From this list, we removed all the papers which contained any of the above phrases in their title because this would make the clustering task easy. The pruned list contains 1190 papers. We manually classified each paper into four classes (Dependency Parsing, Machine Translation, Summarization, Other) by considering the full text of the paper. The manually cleaned data set consists of 275 Machine Translation papers, 73 Dependency Parsing papers and 32 Summarization papers. Table 1 lists a few sample papers from each class.

WebKB(Sen et al., 2008): The data set consists of a subset of the original WebKB data set. The corpus consists of 877 web pages collected from four different universities. Each web page is represented by a 0/1-valued word vector with 1703 unique words after stemming and removing stopwords. All words with document frequency less than 10 were removed.

Cora(Sen et al., 2008): The Cora dataset consists of 2708 scientific publications classified into one of seven classes. The citation network consists of 5429 links. Each publication in the dataset is described by a 0/1-valued word vector indicating the absence/presence of the corresponding word from the dictionary. The dictionary consists of 1433 unique words.

For all the data sets, we constructed two graphs, the kewyord feature graph and the link similarity graph. The keyword feature layer graph, $G_f = (V_f, E_f, w_f)$ is a weighted graph where V_f is the set of all features. The edge weight between keywords f_i and f_j represents the similarity between the features. The edge weights are initialized to the cosine similarity between their corresponding document vectors. The link similarity graph, $G_o = (V_o, E_o, w_o)$ is another weighted graph where V_o is the set of objects. The edge weight represents the similarity between the documents and is initialized to the similarity between the documents due to the link structure. The link similarity between two documents is computed using the similarity measure proposed by (Harel and Koren, 2001) on the citation graph. We also performed experiments by initializing the similarity between documents to the keyword similarity. Although, our algorithm still outperforms other algorithms and the baselines (not shown due to space restrictions), the accuracy using citation similarity is higher.

7 Results and Discussion

Figure 1 shows the accuracy of the classification obtained using different similarity measures. It can be seen that the proposed algorithm (both the variants) performs much better than other similarity measures by a large margin. The algorithm performs much better when more information is provided in the form of TF-IDF scores. We attribute this to the rich representation of the data. In our algorithm, the data is represented as a set of heterogeneous graphs (layers) which are connected together instead of the normal feature vector representation. Thus, we can leverage on the similarity between the keywords and the objects (documents) to iteratively improve similarity in both layers. Whereas, in the case of the algorithm in (Zhou and Burges, 2007) all the graphs are isolated homogeneous graphs. Hence there is no information transfer across the different graphs.

For the clustering task, we use Normalized Mutual Information (NMI) (Strehl and Ghosh, 2002) between the ground truth clusters and the outputted clustering as the measure of clustering accuracy.

Table 2 shows the Normalized Mutual Information scores obtained by the different similarity measures on the different data sets.

8 Conclusion

In this paper, we have proposed a novel approach to compute similarity between documents and keywords iteratively. We formalized the problem of similarity estimation as an optimization problem induced by a regularization framework over edges in multiple graphs. We propose an efficient, iterative algorithm based on Alternating Optimization (AO) which has a neat, intuitive interpretation in terms of random walks over multiple graphs. We demonstrated the improved performance of the proposed algorithm over many different baselines and a state-of-the-art classifcation algorithm and a similarity measure which uses the same information as given to our algorithm.

Similarity Measure	AAN	Texas	Wisconsin	Washington	Cornell	Cora
Content Similarity (Cosine)	0.66	0.34	0.42	0.59	0.63	0.48
Link Similarity	0.45	0.49	0.39	0.52	0.56	0.52
Linear Combination	0.69	0.54	0.46	0.54	0.68	0.54
Unified Similarity	0.78	0.69	0.54	0.66	0.72	0.64
Unified Similarity-Binary	0.80	0.68	0.56	0.69	0.74	0.66
Unified Similarity-TFIDF	**0.84**	**0.70**	**0.60**	**0.72**	**0.78**	**0.70**

Table 2: Normalized Mutual Information scores of the different similarity measures on the different data sets

References

Francis R. Bach, Gert R. G. Lanckriet, and Michael I. Jordan. 2004. Multiple kernel learning, conic duality, and the smo algorithm. In *Proceedings of the twenty-first international conference on Machine learning*, ICML '04, pages 6–, New York, NY, USA. ACM.

James Bezdek and Richard Hathaway. 2002. Some notes on alternating optimization. In Nikhil Pal and Michio Sugeno, editors, *Advances in Soft Computing AFSS 2002*, volume 2275 of *Lecture Notes in Computer Science*, pages 187–195. Springer Berlin.

Peter F. Brown, John Cocke, Stephen A. Della Pietra, Vincent J. Della Pietra, Fredrick Jelinek, John D. Lafferty, Robert L. Mercer, and Paul S. Roossin. 1990. A statistical approach to machine translation. *Computational Linguistics*.

Corinna Cortes, Mehryar. Mohri, and Afshin Rostamizadeh. 2009. Learning non-linear combinations of kernels. In *In NIPS*.

Inderjit S. Dhillon, Subramanyam Mallela, and Dharmendra S. Modha. 2003. Information-theoretic co-clustering. In *Proceedings of the ninth ACM SIGKDD international conference on Knowledge discovery and data mining*, KDD '03, pages 89–98, New York, NY, USA. ACM.

Inderjit S. Dhillon, Yuqiang Guan, and Brian Kulis. 2007. Weighted graph cuts without eigenvectors a multilevel approach. *IEEE Transactions on Pattern Analysis and Machine Intelligence*, 29(11):1944–1957, November.

William A. Gale and Kenneth Ward Church. 1991. A program for aligning sentences in bilingual corpora. In *In Proceedings of ACL*.

David Harel and Yehuda Koren. 2001. On clustering using random walks. In *Foundations of Software Technology and Theoretical Computer Science 2245*, pages 18–41. Springer-Verlag.

Daniel Marcu and William Wong. 2002. A phrase-based, joint probability model for statistical machine translation. In *In Proceedings of EMNLP*.

Pradeep Muthukrishnan, Dragomir Radev, and Qiaozhu Mei. 2010. Edge weight regularization over multiple graphs for similarity learning. In *In ICDM*.

Ted Pedersen, Siddharth Patwardhan, and Jason Michelizzi. 2004. Wordnet::similarity: measuring the relatedness of concepts. In *Demonstration Papers at HLT-NAACL 2004*, HLT-NAACL–Demonstrations '04, pages 38–41, Stroudsburg, PA, USA. Association for Computational Linguistics.

Dragomir R. Radev, Pradeep Muthukrishnan, and Vahed Qazvinian. 2009. The ACL Anthology Network corpus. In *In Proceedings of the ACL Workshop on Natural Language Processing and Information Retrieval for Digital Libraries*.

Prithviraj Sen, Galileo Mark Namata, Mustafa Bilgic, Lise Getoor, Brian Gallagher, and Tina Eliassi-Rad. 2008. Collective classification in network data. *AI Magazine*, 29(3):93–106.

Alexander Strehl and Joydeep Ghosh. 2002. Cluster ensembles: a knowledge reuse framework for combining partitionings. In *Eighteenth national conference on Artificial intelligence*, pages 93–98, Menlo Park, CA, USA. American Association for Artificial Intelligence.

Dengyong Zhou and Christopher J. C. Burges. 2007. Spectral clustering and transductive learning with multiple views. In *ICML '07*, pages 1159–1166, New York, NY, USA.

Xiaojin Zhu, Zoubin Ghahramani, and John Lafferty. 2003. Semi-supervised learning using gaussian fields and harmonic functions. In *ICML 2003*, pages 912–919.

Unrestricted Quantifier Scope Disambiguation

Mehdi Manshadi and James Allen
Department of Computer Science, University of Rochester
Rochester, NY, 14627, USA
{mehdih,james}@cs.rochester.edu

Abstract

We present the first work on applying statistical techniques to unrestricted Quantifier Scope Disambiguation (QSD), where there is no restriction on the type or the number of quantifiers in the sentence. We formulate unrestricted QSD as learning to build a Directed Acyclic Graph (DAG) and define evaluation metrics based on the properties of DAGs. Previous work on statistical scope disambiguation is very limited, only considering sentences with two explicitly quantified noun phrases (NPs). In addition, they only handle a restricted list of quantifiers. In our system, all NPs, explicitly quantified or not (e.g. definites, bare singulars/plurals, etc.), are considered for possible scope interactions. We present early results on applying a simple model to a small corpus. The preliminary results are encouraging, and we hope will motivate further research in this area.

1 Introduction

There are at least two interpretations for the following sentence:

(1) *Every line ends with a digit.*

In one reading, there is a unique digit (say 2) at the end of all lines. This is the case where the quantifier *A outscopes* (aka having *wide-scope* over) the quantifier *Every*. The other case is the one in which *Every* has *wide-scope* (or alternatively *A* has *narrow-scope*), and represents the reading in which different lines could possibly end with distinct digits. This phenomenon is known as *quantifier scope ambiguity*.

Shortly after the first efforts to build natural language understanding systems, Quantifier Scope Disambiguation (QSD) was realized to be very difficult. Woods (1978) was one of the first to suggest a way to get around this problem. He presented a framework for scope-underspecified semantic representation. He suggests representing the Logical Form (LF) of the above sentence as:

(2) *<Every x Line>*
<A y Digit>
Ends-with(x, y)

in which, the relative scope of the quantifiers is underspecified. Since then *scope underspecification* has been the most popular way to deal with quantifier scope ambiguity in deep language understanding systems (e.g. Boxer (Bos 2004), TRAINS (Allen et al. 2007), BLUE (Clark and Harrison 2008), and DELPH-IN[1]). Scope underspecification works in practice, only because many NLP applications (e.g. machine translation) could be achieved without quantifier scope disambiguation. QSD on the other hand, is critical for many other NLP tasks such as question answering systems, dialogue systems and computing entailment.

Almost all efforts in the 80s and 90s on QSD adopt heuristics based on the lexical properties of the quantifiers, syntactic/semantic properties of the sentences, and discourse/pragmatic cues (VanLehn

[1] http://www.delph-in.net/

1978, Moran 1988, Alshawi 1992). For example, it is widely known that in English, the quantifier *each* tends to have the widest scope. Also, the subject of a sentence often outscopes the direct object.[2] In cases where these heuristics conflict, (manually) weighted preference rules are adopted to resolve the conflict (Hurum 1988, , Pafel 1997).

In the last decade there has been some effort to apply statistical and machine learning (ML) techniques to QSD. All the previous efforts, however, suffer from the following two limitations (see section 2 for details):

- They only allow scoping two NPs per sentence.
- The NPs must be explicitly quantified (e.g. they ignore definites or bare singulars/plurals), and the quantifiers are restricted to a predefined list.

In this paper, we present the first work on applying statistical techniques to unrestricted QSD, where we put no restriction on the type or the number of NPs to be scoped in a sentence. In fact, every two NPs, explicitly quantified or not (including definites, indefinites, bare singulars/plurals, pronouns, etc.), are examined for possible scope interactions. Scoping only two quantifiers per sentence, the previous work defines QSD as a single classification task (e.g. 0 where the first quantifier has wide-scope, and 1 otherwise). As a result standard metrics for classification tasks are used for evaluation purposes. We formalize the unrestricted form of QSD as learning to build a DAG over the set of NP chunks in the sentence. We define accuracy, precision and recall metrics based on the properties of DAGs for evaluation purposes.

We report the application of our model to a small corpus. As seen later, the early results are promising and shall motivate further research on applying ML techniques to unrestricted QSD. In fact, they set a baseline for future work in this area.

The structure of this paper is as follows. Section (2) reviews the related work. In (3) we briefly describe our corpus. We formalize the problem of quantifier scope disambiguation for multiple quantifiers in section (4) and define some evaluation metrics in (5). (6) presents our model including the kinds of features we have used. We present our experiments in (7) and give a discussion of the results in (8). (9) summarizes the current work and gives some directions for the future work.

[2] Allen (1995) discusses some of these heuristics and gives an algorithm to incorporate those for scoping while parsing.

2 Related work

Earlier we mentioned that a standard approach to deal with quantifier scope ambiguity is scope underspecification. More recent underspecification formalisms such as Hole Semantics (Bos 1996), Minimal Recursion Semantics (Copestake et al. 2001), and Dominance Constraints (Egg et al. 2001), present constraint-based frameworks. Every constraint forces one term to be in the scope of another, hence filters out some of the possible readings. For example, one may add a constraint to an underspecified representation (UR) to force island constraints. Constraints can be added incrementally to the UR as the sentence processing goes deeper (e.g. at the discourse and/or pragmatic level). The main drawback with these formalisms is that they only allow for hard constraints; that is every scope-resolved representation must satisfy all the constraints in order to be a valid interpretation of the sentence. In practice, however, most constraints that can be drawn from discourse or pragmatic knowledge have a soft nature; that is, they describe a scope preference that is allowed to be violated, though at a cost.

Motivated by the above problem, Koller et al. (2008) define an underspecified scope representation based on regular tree grammars, which allows for both hard constraints and weighted soft constraints. They present a PCFG-style algorithm that computes the reading, which satisfies all the hard constraints and has the maximum product of the weights. However, they assume that the weights are already given. Their algorithm, for example, can be used in traditional QSD approaches with weighted heuristics to systematically compute the best reading. The main question though is how to automatically learn those weights. One solution is using corpus-based methods to learn soft constraints and the cost associated with their violation, in terms of *features* and their *weights*.

To the best of our knowledge, there have been three major efforts on statistical scope disambiguation for English. Higgins and Sadock (2003), hence HS03, is the first work among these systems. They define a list of quantifiers that they consider for scope disambiguation. This list does not include definites, indefinites, and many other challenging scope phenomena. They extract all sentences from the Wall Street journal section of the Penn Treebank, containing exactly two quantifiers from this list. This forms a corpus of 890 sentences, each labeled with the relative scope of the two quantifiers, with the possibility of no scope interaction. The no scope interaction case happens to be the majority class in their corpus and includes more than 61% of the sentences, defining a baseline for their QSD system. They achieve the inter-annotator agreement of only 52% on this task.

They treat QSD as a classification task with three possible classes (*wide scope*, *narrow scope*, and *no scope interaction*). Three forms of feature are incorporated into the classifier: part-of-speech (POS) tags, lexical features, and syntactic properties. Several classification models including naïve Bayes classifier, maximum entropy classifier, and single-layer perceptron are tested, among which the single-layer perceptron performs the best, with the accuracy of 77%.

Galen and MacCartney (2004), hence GM04, build a corpus of 305 sentences from LSAT and GRE logic games, each containing exactly two quantifiers from an even more restricted list of quantifiers. They use an additional label for the case where the two scopings are equivalent (as in the case of two existentials). In around 70% of the sentences in their corpus, the first quantifier has wide scope, defining a majority class baseline of 70% for their QSD system.[3] Three classifiers are tried: naïve Bayes, logistics regression, and support vector machine (SVM), among which SVM performs the best and achieves the accuracy of 94%.

In a recent work, Srinivasan and Yates (2009) study the usage of pragmatic knowledge in finding the preferred scoping of natural language sentences. The sentences are all extracted from 5-grams in Web1Tgram (from Google, Inc) and share the same syntactic structure: an active voice English sentence of the form *(S (NP (V (NP | PP))))*. For the task of finding the most preferred reading, they annotate 46 sentences, each containing two quantifiers: *Every* and *A*, where the first quantifier is always *A*. Each sentence is annotated with one of the two labels (*Every* has wide scope or not). They use a totally different approach for finding the preferred reading. The n-grams in Web1Tgram are used to extract relations such as *Live(Person, City)*, and to estimate the expected cardinality of the two classes, which form the arguments of the relation, that is *Person* and *City*.

> 1. *Print [1/ every line] of [2/ the file] that starts with [3/ a digit] followed by [4/ punctuation].*
>
>   *QSD: {2>1, 2>3, 1>3, 2>4, 1>4}*
>
> 2. *Delete [1/ the first character] of [2/ every word] and [3/ the first word] of [4/ every line] in [5/ the file].*
>
>   *QSD: {5>4, 5>3, 4>3, 5>2, 5>1, 2>1}*
>
> Figure 1. Two NP-chunked sentences with QSDs

They decide on the preferred scoping by comparing the size of the two classes, achieving the accuracy of 74% on their test set. The main advantage of this work is that it is open domain.

3 Our corpus

The fact that HS03, in spite of ignoring challenging scope phenomena and scoping only two quantifiers per sentence, achieve the IAA of 52% shows how hard scope disambiguation could be for humans. It becomes enormously more challenging when there is no restriction on the type or the number of quantifiers in the sentence, especially when NPs without explicit quantifiers such as definites, indefinites, and bare singulars/plurals are taken into account. As a matter of fact, our own early effort to annotate part of the Penn Treebank with full scope information soon proved to be too ambitious. Instead, we picked a domain that covers most challenging phenomena in scope disambiguation, while keeping the scope disambiguation fairly intuitive. This made building the first corpus of English text with full quantifier scope information feasible. Our domain of choice is the description of tasks about editing plain text files, in other words, a natural language interface for text editors such as SED, AWK, or EMACS. Figure (1) gives some sentences from the corpus. The reason behind scoping in this domain being fairly intuitive is that given any of these sentences, a conscious knowledge of scoping is critical in order to be able to accomplish the explained task.

Our corpus consists of 500 sentences manually extracted from the web. The sentences have been labeled with gold standard NP chunks, where each NP chunk has been indexed with a number 1 through n (n is the number of chunks in the sentence). The annotators are asked to use outscoping relations represented by '>' to specify the relative scope of every pair $1 \leq i,j \leq n$, with an option to leave

[3] They do not report any inter-annotator agreement.

the pair *unscoped*. For example a relation *(2>3)* states that the second NP in the sentence *outscopes* (aka *dominates*) the third NP. Since outscoping relation is *transitive*, for the convenience of the annotation, the outscoping relations are allowed to be cascaded forming dominance chains. For example, the scoping for the sentence 2 in figure (1) can alternatively be represented as shown in (3).

(3) (5>2>1 ; 5>4>3)

As a result, every pair *<i,j>* ($1 \le i < j \le n$) is implicitly labeled with one of the three labels:

i. *Wide scope:* either explicitly given by the annotator as *i>j* or implied using the transitive property of outscoping[4]
ii. *Narrow scope:* either explicitly given by the annotator as *j>i* or implied using the transitive property of outscoping
iii. *No interaction:* where neither wide scope nor narrow scope could be inferred from the given scoping.[5]

We achieved the IAA of 75% (based on Cohen's kappa score) on this corpus, significantly better than the 52% IAA of HS03, especially considering the fact that we put no restriction on the type of the quantification. Our sentence-level IAA is around 66%. The details of the corpus, and the annotation scheme are beyond the scope of this paper and can be found in Manshadi et al. (2011).

4 Formalization

Outscoping is an *anti-symmetric transitive* relation, so it defines an *order* over the chunks. Since we do not force every two chunks to be involved in an outscoping relation, QSD defines a *partial order* over the NP chunks. Formally,

Definition 1: Given a sentence S with NP chunks *1..n*, a relation *P* over *{1..n}* is called a *QSD* for S, if and only if *P* is a partial order.

Definition 2: Given a sentence S with NP chunks *1..n*, and the QSD *P*, we say (chunk) *i outscopes* (chunk) *j* if and only if $(i>j) \in P$.

[4] That is if *i* outscopes *j* and *j* outscopes *k* then *i* outscopes *k*.

[5] The no interaction class includes two cases: no scope interaction and logical equivalence which means we follow the three-label scheme of HS03 as opposed to the four-label scheme of GM04. This is because when there is a logical equivalence, except for trivial cases, there are no clear criteria based on which one can decide whether there is a scope interaction or not. Furthermore, distinguishing these two cases does not make much difference in practice.

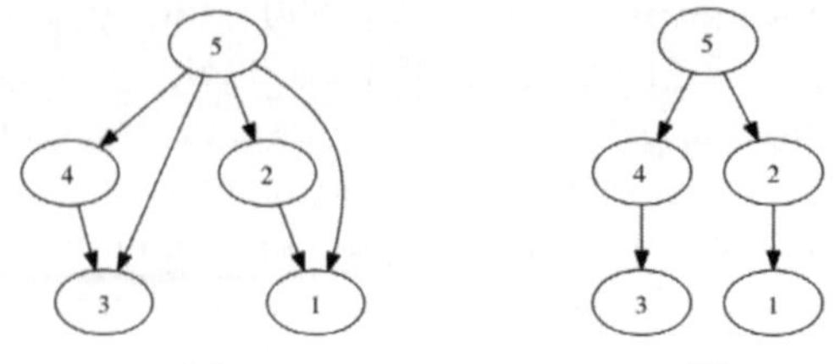

(a) (b)

Figure 2. Scopings represented as DAGs

Definition 3: Given a sentence S with NP chunks *1..n*, and the QSD *P*, chunk *i* is said to be *disjoint* with chunk *j* if and only if

$$(i>j) \notin P \wedge (j>i) \notin P.$$

4.1 QSD and directed acyclic graphs

Partial orders can be represented using *Directed Acyclic Graphs* (*DAGs*) in which *dominance* (aka *reachability*) determines the order. More precisely, every DAG *G* over *n* nodes $v_1..v_n$ defines a partial order P_G over the set $\{v_1..v_n\}$ in which, v_i precedes v_j in P_G if and only if v_i *dominates*[6] v_j in *G*.

Definition 4: Given a sentence S with NP chunks *1..n*, every DAG *G* over *n* nodes (labeled *1…n*) defines a QSD P_G for S, such that

$$(i>j) \in P_G \Leftrightarrow i \text{ dominates } j \text{ in } G$$

For example figure (2a,b) represent the DAGs corresponding to the QSD of sentence 2 in figure (1) and the QSD in (3) respectively. Following definition 3 and 4, the no interaction relation defined in section (3) translates to corresponding nodes in the DAG being *disjoint*[7]. Therefore the three types of scope interaction defined in *i, ii*, and *iii* (section 3), translate to the following relations in a DAG.

(4) Wide Scope (WS): i dominates j
Narrow Scope (NS): j dominates i
No Interaction (NI): i and j are disjoint.

5 Evaluation metrics

Intuitively the similarity of two QSDs, given for a sentence S, can be defined as the ratio of the chunk pairs that have the same label in both QSDs to the total number of pairs. For example, consider the

[6] Given a DAG *G=(V, E)*, node *u* is said to immediately dominate node *v* if and only if $(u,v) \in E$. "dominates" is the *reflexive transitive* closure of "immediately dominates".

[7] The nodes *u* and *v* of the DAG *G* are said to be disjoint if neither *u* dominates *v* nor *v* dominates *u*.

two DAGs in figure (2). Although looking different, both DAGs define the same partial order (i.e. QSD). This is because the partial order represented by a DAG G corresponds to the *transitive closure* (*TC*) of G.

5.1 Transitive closure

The transitive closure of G, shown as G^+, is defined as follows:

(5) $G^+ = \{(i,j) \mid i \text{ dominates } j \text{ in } G\}$

For example, figure (2a) is the transitive closure of the DAG in figure (2b). Given this, the similarity metric mentioned above can be formally defined as the number of (unordered) pairs of node that match between G_1^+ and G_2^+ divided by the total number of (unordered) pairs.

Definition 5: Similarity measure or σ.
Given sentence S with n NP chunks and two scopings represented by DAGs G_1 and G_2, we define:

$$M(G_1, G_2) = \{ \{i,j\} \mid ((i,j) \in G_1^+ \wedge (i,j) \in G_2^+) \vee ((j,i) \in G_1^+ \wedge (j,i) \in G_2^+) \vee ((i,j),(j,i) \notin G_1^+ \wedge (i,j),(j,i) \notin G_2^+) \}$$

$$\sigma(G_1, G_2) = 2|M(G_1, G_2)| / [n(n-1)]$$

Where $|.|$ represents the cardinality of a set. σ is a value between 0 and 1 (inclusive) where 1 means that the QSDs are equivalent and 0 means that they do not agree on the label of any pair. σ is useful for measuring the similarity of two scope annotations when calculating IAA. It can also be used as an *accuracy* metric for evaluating an automatic scope disambiguation system where the similarity of a predicted QSD is calculated respect to a gold standard QSD. In fact, if $n=2$, σ is equivalent to the metric that HS03 use to evaluate their system.

The similarity metric defined above has some disadvantages. For example, HS03 report that more than 61% of the scope relations in their corpus are of type no interaction. Using this metric, a model that leaves everything unscoped has more than 61% percent accuracy on their corpus! In fact, the output of a QSD system on pairs with no interaction is not practically important.[8] What is more important is to recover the pairs with scope interaction correctly. The standard way to address this is to define precision/recall metrics.

Definition 6: Precision and Recall (TC version)
Given the gold standard DAG G_g and the predicted DAG G_p, we define the precision (P) and the recall (R) as follows:

$$TP = |\{ (i,j) \mid (i,j) \in G_p^+ \wedge (i,j) \in G_g^+ \}|$$
$$N = |\{ (i,j) \mid (i,j) \in G_p^+ \}|$$
$$M = |\{ (i,j) \mid (i,j) \in G_g^+ \}|$$
$$P = TP / N$$
$$R = TP / M$$

5.2 Transitive reduction

The TC-based metrics implicitly count some matching pairs more than once. For example, if in both QSDs we have 1>2 and 2>3, then 1>3 is implied, so counting it as another match is redundant and favors toward higher accuracies. Naturally, there are so many redundancies in TC. To address this issue, we define another set of metrics based on the concept of *transitive reduction* (TR). Given a directed graph G, the transitive reduction of G, represented as G^-, is intuitively a graph with the same reachability (i.e. dominance) relation but with no redundant edges. More formally, the transitive reduction of G is a graph G^- such that

- $(G^-)^+ = G^+$
- $\forall G', \ (G')^+ = G^+ \Rightarrow |G^-| \leq |G'|$

For example, figure (2b) represents the transitive reduction of the DAG in figure (2a). Fortunately if a directed graph is acyclic, its transitive reduction is unique (Aho et al., 1972). Therefore, defining TR-based precision/recall metrics is valid.

Definition 7: Precision and Recall (TR version)
Simply replace every '+' in definition 6 with a '-'.

6 The model

We extend HS03's approach for scoping two NPs per sentence to the general case of n NPs. Every pair of chunks $<i,j>$ (where $1 \leq i < j \leq n$) is treated as an independent sample to be classified as one of the three classes defined in (3), that is *WS*, *NS*, or *NI*. Therefore a sentence with n NP chunks consists of $C(n, 2) = n(n-1)/2$ samples. The average

[8] In practice the target language is often first order logic or a variant of that. When a pair is labeled *NI* in gold standard data, if there exist valid interpretations (satisfying hard constraints) in which either of the two quantifiers can be in the scope of the other, then the ordering of this pair does not matter; that is switching the order of such pairs result in equivalent formulas.

1. *Print [1/ every/D line/H] of [2/ the/D file/H] that starts with [3/ two/CD digits/H/S] followed by [4/ punctuation/H].*

2. *Delete [1/ the/D first character/H] of [2/ every/D word/H] and [3/ the/D first word/H] of [4/ every/D line/H] in [5/ the/D file/H].*

Figure 3. Labeling determiners and head nouns

number of NPs per sentence in the corpus is 3.7, so the corpus provides 1850 samples. Since the scoping of each pair is predicted independent of the other pairs in the sentence, it may result in an ill-formed scoping, i.e. a scoping with cycles. As explained later, this case did not happen in our corpus. A *MultiClass SVM* (Crammer et al. 2001), referred to as *SVM-MC* in the rest of the paper, is used as the classifier. We provide more supervision by annotating data with the following labels.

I. Determiner features

For every NP chunk, we tag pre-determiner (/PD), determiner (/D), possessive determiner (/POS), and number (/CD) (if they exist) as part of the determiner (see figure 3). Given the pair *<i,j>*, for either of the chunks *i* and *j,* and every tag mentioned above, we use a binary feature, which shows whether this tag exists in that chunk or not. For tags that do exist (except /CD) the lexical word is also used as a feature.

II. Semantic head features

We tag the semantic head of the NP and use its lexical word as feature. Also the plurality of the NP (/S tag for plurals) is used as a binary feature.

III. 3. Dependency features

The above two sets of feature are about the individual properties of the chunks. But this last category represents how each NP contributes to the semantics of the whole sentence. We borrow from Manshadi et al. (2009) the concept of *Dependency Graph* (*DG*), which encodes this information in a compact way. DG represents the argument structure of the predicates that form the logical form of a sentence. The DG of a sentence with n NP chunks contains $n+1$ nodes labeled $0..n$. Node i ($i>0$) represents the predicate or the conjunction of the predicates that describes the NP chunk i, and node 0 represents the main predicate (or conjunction of predicates) of the sentence. An edge from i

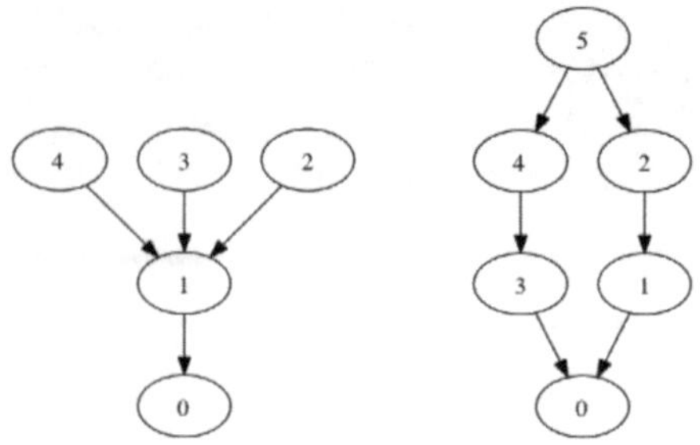

(a) (b)

Figure 4. Dependency Graphs for figure (3) sentences

to j shows that chunk i is an argument of a predicate represented by node j.

For example, in sentence (1) of figure (3), chunk 1 is clearly the argument of the verb *Print* (the main predicate of the sentence), therefore there is an edge from 1 to 0 in the DG of this sentence as shown in figure (4a). Also, chunks 2..4 are part of the description of chunk 1, so they are the arguments of the predicate(s) describing chunk 1. This means that there must be edges from nodes 2..4 to node 1 in the DG. Similarly for sentence 2 in figure (3), chunk 5 is part of the description (hence an argument of the predicates) of chunks 2 and 4; chunks 2 and 4 are part of the description of 1 and 3 respectively; and 1 and 3 are both arguments of the verb *Delete*, the main predicate of the sentence, resulting in the DG given in figure (4b).

The following features are extracted from the DG for every sample *<i,j>*($1 \le i < j \le n$):

- *Does i (or j) immediately dominate 0?*
- *Does i (or j) immediately dominate j (or i)?*
- *Does i (or j) dominate j (or i)?*
- *Are i,j siblings ?*
- *Do i,j share the same child?*

Note that DG has a close relationship with the dependency tree of a sentence; for example, it shows the dependency relation(s) between a noun or verb and their modifier(s). Therefore it actually encodes some syntactic properties of a sentence.

7 Experiments

100 sentences from the corpus were picked at random as the development set, in order to study the relevant features and their contribution to QSD. The rest of the corpus (400 sentences) was then used to do a 5 fold cross validation. We used *SVM*[Multiclass] from *SVM-light* toolkit (Joachims 1999) as the classifier.

	P	R	F
Baseline (TC)	31.8%	49.7%	38.8%
Baseline (TR)	27.4%	33.9%	30.3%
SVM-MC (TC)	73.0%	**84.7%**	78.4%
SVM-MC (TR)	70.6%	**76.2%**	73.2%

Table 1. Constraint-level results

Before giving the results, we define a baseline. HS03 use the most frequent label as the baseline and the similarity metric given in definition (5) to evaluate the performance. Since more than 61% of the labels in their corpus is *NI*, the baseline system (that leaves every sentence unscoped) has the accuracy above 61%. In our corpus, the majority class is *WS* containing around 35% of the samples. *NS* and *NI* each contain 34% and 31% of the samples respectively. This means that there is a slight tendency for having scope preference in chronological order. Therefore, the linear order of the chunks (i.e. from left to right) defines a reasonable baseline.
The results of our experiments are shown in table 1. The table lists the parameters *P*, *R*, and *F*-score[9] for our SVM-MC model vs. the baseline system. For each system, two sets of metrics have been reported: TC-based and TR-based.

Table 2 lists the sentence-level accuracy of the system. We computed two metrics for sentence-level accuracy: *Acc* and *Acc-EZ*. In calculating *Acc*, a sentence is considered correct if all the labels (including *NI*) exactly match the gold standard labels. However, this is an unnecessarily tough metric. As mentioned before (footnote 8), in practice the output of the system for the samples labeled *NI* is not important; all we care is that all *outscoping* (i.e. *WS/NS*) relations are recovered correctly. In other words, in practice, the system's recall is the most important parameter. Regarding this fact, we define *Acc-EZ* as the percentage of sentences with 100% recall (ignoring the value of precision).

In order to compare our system with that of HS03, we applied our model unmodified to their corpus using the same set-up, a 10-fold cross validation. However, since their corpus is not annotated with DG, we translated our dependency features to the properties of the Penn Treebank's phrase structure trees. Table (3) lists the accuracy

[9] F-score is defined as $F=2PR/(P+R)$.

	Acc	*Acc-EZ*
Baseline	27.0%	43.8%
SVM-MC	62.3%	78.0%

Table 2. Sentence level accuracy

of their best model, their baseline, and our SVM-MC model. As seen in this table, their model outperforms ours. This, however, is not surprising. First, although we trained our model on their corpus, the feature engineering of our model was done based on our own development set. Second, since our corpus is not annotated with phrase structure trees, our model does not use any of their features that can only be extracted from phrase structure trees. It remains for future work to incorporate the features extracted from phrase structure trees (which is not already encoded in DG) and evaluate the performance of the model on either corpus.

8 Discussion

As seen in tables 1 and 2, for a first effort at full quantifier scope disambiguation, the results are promising. The constraint-based F-score of 78% is already higher than the inter-annotator agreement, which is 75% (measured using the TC based similarity metric; see definition 5). Furthermore, our system outperforms the baseline, by more than 40% (judging by the constraint-based F-score). This is significant, comparing to the work of HS03, which outperforms the baseline by 16%.

We mentioned before that in our corpus in average there are around 4 NPs per sentence resulting in 6 samples per sentence. Therefore the chance of predicting all the labels correctly is very slim. However, the baseline (i.e. the left to right order) does a good job and predicts the correct QSD for 27% of the sentences. At the sentence level, our model does not reach the IAA, but the performance (62%) is not much lower than the IAA (66%).

A question may arise that since the model treats

	σ
Baseline	61.1%
HS04	**77.0%**
Our Model	73.3%

Table 3. Comparison with HS04 system on their dataset

the pairs of NP independently, what guarantees that the scopings are valid; that is the predicted directed graphs are in fact DAGs. For example, for a sentence with 3 NP chunks, the classifier may predict that 1>2, 2>3, and 3>1, which results in a loop! As a matter of fact, there is nothing in the model that guarantees the validness of the predicted scopings. In spite of that, surprisingly all generated graphs in our tests were in fact DAGs! In order to explain this fact, we run two experiments. In the first experiment, corresponding to every sentence S in the corpus with *n* chunks, we generated a random directed graph over *n* nodes. Only 10% of the graphs had cycles. It means that more than 90% of randomly generated directed graphs with *n* nodes (where the distribution of *n* is its distribution in our corpus) are acyclic. In the second experiment, for every sentence with *n* chunks, we created the samples <*i,j*> by randomly selecting values for all the features. We then tested the classifier in our original set-up, a 5-fold cross validation. In this case, only 4% of the sentences were assigned inconsistent labeling. This means that chances of having a loop in the scoping are small even when the classifier is trained on samples with randomly valued features, therefore it is not surprising that a classifier trained on the actual data learns some useful structures which make the chance of assigning inconsistent labels very slim.

In general, if the classifier predicts such inconsistent scopings, the PCFG-style algorithm of Koller et al. (2008) comes handy in order to find a valid scoping with the highest weight.

9 Summary and future work

We presented the first work on unrestricted statistical scope disambiguation in which all NP chunks in a sentence are considered for possible scope interactions. We defined the task of full scope disambiguation as assigning a directed acyclic graph over *n* nodes to a sentence with *n* NP chunks. We then defined some metrics for evaluation purposes based on the two well-known concepts for DAGs: transitive closure and transitive reduction.

We use a simple model for automatic QSD. Our model treats QSD as a ternary classification task on every pair of NP chunks. A multiclass SVM together with some POS, lexical and dependency features is used to do the classification. We apply this model to a corpus of English text in the domain of editing plain text files, which has been annotated with full scope information. The preliminary results reach the F-score of 73% (based on transitive reduction metrics) at the constraint level and the accuracy of 62% at the sentence level. The system outperforms the baseline by a high margin (43% at the constraint level and 35% at the sentence level).

Our ternary SVM-based classification model is a preliminary model, used for justification of our theoretical framework. Many improvements are possible, for example, directly predicting the whole DAG as a structured output. Also, the features that we use are rather basic. There are other linguistically motivated features that can be incorporated, e.g. some properties of the phrase structure trees, not already encoded in dependency graphs.

Another problem with the current system is that the extra supervision has been provided by manually labeling the data (e.g. with dependency graphs). This could be done automatically by applying off the shelf parsers or POS taggers, possibly by adapting them to our domain.

Although we consider all NPs for scope resolution, scopal operators such as *negation*, *modal/logical* operators have been ignored in this work. We also do not distinguish *distributive* vs. *collective* reading of plurals in the current system.[10] Incorporating scopal operators and handling distributivity vs. collectivity would be the next step in expanding this work.

Finally, since hand annotation of scope information is very challenging, applying semi-supervised or even unsupervised techniques to QSD is very demanding. In fact, leveraging unlabeled data to do QSD seems quite promising. This is because domain dependent knowledge plays a critical role in scope disambiguation and this knowledge can be learned from unlabeled data using unsupervised methods.

Acknowledgement

We would like to thank Derrick Higgins for providing us with the HS03's corpus. This work was supported in part by grants from the National Science Foundation (IIS-1012205) and The Office of Naval Research (N000141110417).

[10] The corpus has already been annotated with all this information, but our QSD model is not designed for such a comprehensive scope disambiguation.

References

Aho, A., Garey, M., Ullman, J. (1972). *The Transitive Reduction of a Directed Graph.* SIAM Journal on Computing 1 (2): 131–137.

Allen, J. (1995) *Natural Langue Understanding*, Benjamin-Cummings Publishing Co., Inc.

Allen, J., Dzikovska, M., Manshadi, M., Swift, M. (2007) *Deep linguistic processing for spoken dialogue systems.* Proceedings of the ACL-07 Workshop on Deep Linguistic Processing, pp. 49-56.

Alshawi, H. (ed.) (1992) *The core language Engine.* Cambridge, MA, MIT Press.

Bos, J., S. Clark, M. Steedman, J. R. Curran, and J. Hockenmaier (2004). *Wide-coverage semantic representations from a CCG parser.* In Proceedings of COLING 2004, Geneva, Switzerland, pp. 1240–1246.

Bos, J. (1996) *Predicate logic unplugged.* In Proc. 10th Amsterdam Colloquium, pages 133–143.

Clark P., Harrison, P. (2008) *Boeing's NLP system and the challenges of semantic representation*, Semantics in Text Processing. STEP 2008.

Copestake, A., Lascarides, A. and Flickinger, D. (2001) *An Algebra for Semantic Construction in Constraint-Based Grammars.* ACL-01. Toulouse, France.

Crammer, K., Y. Singer, N. Cristianini , J. Shawe-taylor, B. Williamson (2001). *On the Algorithmic Implementation of Multi-class SVMs*, Journal of Machine Learning Research.

Egg M., Koller A., and Niehren J. (2001) *The constraint language for lambda structures.* Journal of Logic, Language, and Information, 10:457–485.

Galen, A. and MacCartney, B. (2004). Statistical resolution of scope ambiguity in Natural language. http://nlp.stanford.edu/nlkr/scoper.pdf.

Higgins, D. and Sadock, J. (2003). *A machine learning approach to modeling scope preferences.* Computational Linguistics, 29(1).

Hurum, S. O. (1988) *Handling scope ambiguities in English.* In Proceeding of the second conference on Applied Natural Language Processing (ANLC '88).

Koller, A., Michaela, R., Thater, S. (2008) *Regular Tree Grammars as a Formalism for Scope Underspecification.* ACL-08, Columbus, USA.

Joachims, T. (1999) *Making Large-Scale SVM Learning Practical.* Advances in Kernel Methods - Support Vector Learning, B. Schölkopf and C. Burges and A. Smola (ed.), MIT Press.

Manshadi, M., Allen J., and Swift, M. (2009) *An Efficient Enumeration Algorithm for Canonical Form Underspecified Semantic Representations.* Proceedings of the 14th Conference on Formal Grammar (FG 2009), Bordeaux, France July 25-26.

Moran, D. B. (1988). *Quantifier scoping in the SRI core language engine.* In Proceedings of the 26th Annual Meeting of the Association for Computational Linguistics.

Pafel, J. (1997). *Skopus und logische Struktur. Studien zum Quantorenskopus im Deutschen.* PHD thesis, University of Tübingen.

Srinivasan, P., and Yates, A. (2009). *Quantifier scope disambiguation using extracted pragmatic knowledge: Preliminary results.* In Proceedings of the Conference on Empirical Methods in Natural Language Processing (EMNLP).

VanLehn, K. (1988) *Determining the scope of English quantifiers*, TR AI-TR-483, AI Lab, MIT.

Woods, W. A. (1978) *Semantics and quantification in natural language question answering*, Advances in. Computers, vol. 17, pp 1-87.

From ranked words to dependency trees: two-stage unsupervised non-projective dependency parsing

Anders Søgaard
Center for Language Technology
University of Copenhagen
soegaard@hum.ku.dk

Abstract

Usually unsupervised dependency parsing tries to optimize the probability of a corpus by modifying the dependency model that was presumably used to generate the corpus. In this article we explore a different view in which a dependency structure is among other things a partial order on the nodes in terms of centrality or saliency. Under this assumption we model the partial order directly and derive dependency trees from this order. The result is an approach to unsupervised dependency parsing that is very different from standard ones in that it requires no training data. Each sentence induces a model from which the parse is read off. Our approach is evaluated on data from 12 different languages. Two scenarios are considered: a scenario in which information about part-of-speech is available, and a scenario in which parsing relies only on word forms and distributional clusters. Our approach is competitive to state-of-the-art in both scenarios.

1 Introduction

Unsupervised dependency parsers do not achieve the same quality as supervised or semi-supervised parsers, but in some situations precision may be less important compared to the cost of producing manually annotated data. Moreover, unsupervised dependency parsing is attractive from a theoretical point of view as it does not rely on a particular style of annotation and may potentially provide insights about the difficulties of human language learning.

Unsupervised dependency parsing has seen rapid progress recently, with error reductions on English (Marcus et al., 1993) of about 15% in six years (Klein and Manning, 2004; Spitkovsky et al., 2010), and better and better results for other languages (Gillenwater et al., 2010; Naseem et al., 2010), but results are still far from what can be achieved with small seeds, language-specific rules (Druck et al., 2009) or using cross-language adaptation (Smith and Eisner, 2009; Spreyer et al., 2010).

The standard method in unsupervised dependency parsing is to optimize the overall probability of the corpus by assigning trees to its sentences that capture general patterns in the distribution of part-of-speech (POS). This happens in several iterations over the corpus. This method requires clever initialization, which can be seen as a kind of minimal supervision. State-of-the-art unsupervised dependency parsers, except Seginer (2007), also rely on manually annotated text or text processed by supervised POS taggers. Since there is an intimate relationship between POS tagging and dependency parsing, the POS tags can also be seen as a seed or as partial annotation. Inducing a model from the corpus is typically a very slow process.

This paper presents a new and very different approach to unsupervised dependency parsing. The parser does not induce a model from a big corpus, but with a few exceptions only considers the sentence in question. It *does* use a larger corpus to induce distributional clusters and a ranking of key words in terms of frequency and centrality, but this is computationally efficient and is only indirectly related to the subsequent assignment of dependency structures to sentences. The obvious advantage of not relying on training data is that we do not have to worry about whether the test data reflects the same distribution as the target data (domain adaptation), and since our models are much smaller, parsing will be very fast.

The parser assigns a dependency structure to a sequence of words in two stages. It first decorates the n nodes of what will become our dependency structure with word forms and distributional clusters, constructs a directed acyclic graph from the nodes in $\mathcal{O}(n^2)$, and ranks the nodes using iterative graph-based ranking (Page and Brin, 1998). Subsequently, it constructs a tree from the ranked list of words using a simple $\mathcal{O}(n \log n)$ parsing algorithm.

Our parser is evaluated on the selection of 12 dependency treebanks also used in Gillenwater et al. (2010). We consider two cases: parsing raw text and parsing text with information about POS.

Strictly unsupervised dependency parsing is of course a more difficult problem than unsupervised dependency parsing of manually annotated POS sequences. Nevertheless our *strictly* unsupervised parser, which only sees word forms, performs significantly better than structural baselines, and it outperforms the standard POS-informed DMV-EM model (Klein and Manning, 2004) on 3/12 languages. The full parser, which sees manually annotated text, is competitive to state-of-the-art models such as E-DMV PR AS 140 (Gillenwater et al., 2010).[1]

1.1 Preliminaries

The observed variables in unsupervised dependency parsing are a corpus of sentences $\mathbf{s} = s_1, \ldots, s_n$ where each word w_j in s_i is associated with a POS tag p_j. The hidden variables are dependency structures $\mathbf{t} = t_1, \ldots, t_n$ where s_i labels the vertices of t_i. Each vertex has a single incoming edge, possibly except one called the root of the tree. In this work and in most other work in dependency parsing, we introduce an artificial root node so that all vertices decorated by word forms have an incoming edge.

A dependency structure such as the one in Figure 1 is thus a tree decorated with labels and augmented with a linear order on the nodes. Each edge (i, j) is referred to as a dependency between a head word w_i and a dependent word w_j and sometimes written $w_i \rightarrow w_j$. Let w_0 be the artificial root of the dependency structure. We use $\rightarrow^+$ to denote the transitive closure on the set of edges. Both nodes and edges are typically labeled. Since a dependency structure is a tree, it satisfies the following three constraints: A dependency structure over a sentence $s : w_1, \ldots, w_n$ is *connected*, i.e.:

$$\forall w_i \in s. w_0 \rightarrow^+ w_i$$

A dependency structure is also *acyclic*, i.e.:

$$\neg \exists w_i \in s. w_i \rightarrow^+ w_i$$

Finally, a dependency structure is *single-headed*, i.e.:

$$\forall w_i. \forall w_j. (w_0 \rightarrow w_i \land w_0 \rightarrow w_j) \Rightarrow w_i = w_j$$

If we also require that each vertex other than the artificial root node has an incoming edge we have a complete characterization of dependency structures. In sum, a dependency structure is a tree with a linear order on the leaves where the root of the tree for practical reasons is attached to an artificial root node. The artificial root node makes it easier to implement parsing algorithms.

Finally, we define *projectivity*, i.e. whether the linear order is projective wrt. the dependency tree, as the property of dependency trees that if $w_i \rightarrow w_j$ it also holds that all words in between w_i and w_j are dominated by w_i, i.e. $w_i \rightarrow^+ w_k$. Intuitively, a projective dependency structure contains no crossing edges. Projectivity is not a necessary property of dependency structures. Some dependency structures are projective, others are not. Most if not all previous work in unsupervised dependency parsing has focused on projective dependency parsing, building on work in context-free parsing, but our parser is guaranteed to produce well-formed non-projective dependency trees. Non-projective parsing algorithms for supervised dependency parsing have, for example, been presented in McDonald et al. (2005) and Nivre (2009).

1.2 Related work

Dependency Model with Valence (DMV) by Klein and Manning (2004) was the first unsupervised dependency parser to achieve an accuracy for manually

[1]Naseem et al. (2010) obtain slightly better results, but only evaluate on six languages. They made their code public, though: http://groups.csail.mit.edu/rbg/code/dependency/

POS-tagged English above a right-branching baseline.

DMV is a generative model in which the sentence root is generated and then each head recursively generates its left and right dependents. For each $s_i \in \mathbf{s}$, t_i is assumed to have been built the following way: The arguments of a head h in direction d are generated one after another with the probability that no more arguments of h should be generated in direction d conditioned on h, d and whether this would be the first argument of h in direction d. The POS tag of the argument of h is generated given h and d. Klein and Manning (2004) use expectation maximization (EM) to estimate probabilities with manually tuned linguistically-biased priors.

Smith and Eisner (2005) use contrastive estimation instead of EM, while Smith and Eisner (2006) use structural annealing which penalizes long-distance dependencies initially, gradually weakening the penalty during training. Cohen et al. (2008) use Bayesian priors (Dirichlet and Logistic Normal) with DMV. All of the above approaches to unsupervised dependency parsing build on the linguistically-biased priors introduced by Klein and Manning (2004).

In a similar way Gillenwater et al. (2010) try to penalize models with a large number of distinct dependency types by using sparse posteriors. They evaluate their system on 11 treebanks from the CoNLL 2006 Shared Task and the Penn-III treebank and achieve state-of-the-art performance.

An exception to using linguistically-biased priors is Spitkovsky et al. (2009) who use predictions on sentences of length n to initialize search on sentences of length $n+1$. In other words, their method requires no manual tuning and bootstraps itself on increasingly longer sentences.

A very different, but interesting, approach is taken in Brody (2010) who use methods from unsupervised word alignment for unsupervised dependency parsing. In particular, he sees dependency parsing as directional alignment from a sentence (possible dependents) to itself (possible heads) with the modification that words cannot align to themselves; following Klein and Manning (2004) and the subsequent papers mentioned above, Brody (2010) considers sequences of POS tags rather than raw text. Results are below state-of-the-art, but in some cases better than the DMV model.

2 Ranking dependency tree nodes

The main intuition behind our approach to unsupervised dependency parsing is that the nodes near the root in a dependency structure are in some sense the most important ones. Semantically, the nodes near the root typically express the main predicate and its arguments. Iterative graph-based ranking (Page and Brin, 1998) was first used to rank webpages according to their centrality, but the technique has found wide application in natural language processing. Variations of the algorithm presented in Page and Brin (1998) have been used in keyword extraction and extractive summarization (Mihalcea and Tarau, 2004), word sense disambiguation (Agirre and Soroa, 2009), and abstractive summarization (Ganesan et al., 2010). In this paper, we use it as the first step in a two-step unsupervised dependency parsing procedure.

The parser assigns a dependency structure to a sequence of words in two stages. It first decorates the n nodes of what will become our dependency structure with word forms and distributional clusters, constructs a directed acyclic graph from the nodes in $\mathcal{O}(n^2)$, and ranks the nodes using iterative graph-based ranking. Subsequently, it constructs a tree from the ranked list of words using a simple $\mathcal{O}(n \log n)$ parsing algorithm. This section describes the graph construction step in some detail and briefly describes the iterative graph-based ranking algorithm used.

The first step, however, is assigning distributional clusters to the words in the sentence. We use a hierarchical clustering algorithm to induce 500 clusters from the treebanks using publicly available software.[2] This procedure is quadratic in the number of clusters, but linear in the size of the corpus. The cluster names are bitvectors (see Figure 1).

2.1 Edges

The text graph is now constructed by adding different kinds of directed edges between nodes. The edges are not weighted, but multiple edges between nodes will make transitions between these nodes in

[2] http://www.cs.berkeley.edu/~pliang/software/brown-cluster-1.2.zip

iterative graph-based ranking more likely. The different kinds of edges play the same role in our model as the rule templates in the DMV model, and they are motivated below.

Some of the edge assignments discussed below may seem rather heuristic. The edge template was developed on development data from the English Penn-III treebank (Marcus et al., 1993). Our edge selection was incremental considering first an extended set of candidate edges with arbitrary parameters and then considering each edge type at a time. If the edge type was helpful, we optimized any possible parameters (say context windows) and went on to the next edge type: otherwise we disregarded it.[3] Following data set et al. (2010), we apply the best setting for English to all other languages.

Vine edges. Eisner and Smith (2005) motivate a vine parsing approach to supervised dependency parsing arguing that language users have a strong preference for short dependencies. Reflecting preference for short dependencies, we first add links between all words and their neighbors and neighbors' neighbors. This also guarantees that the final graph is connected.

Keywords and closed class words. We use a keyword extraction algorithm without stop word lists to extract non-content words and the most important content words, typically nouns. The algorithm is a crude simplification of TextRank (Mihalcea and Tarau, 2004) that does not rely on linguistic resources, so that we can easily apply it to low-resource languages. Since we do not use stop word lists, highly ranked words will typically be non-content words, followed by what is more commonly thought of as keywords. Immediate neighbors to top-100 words are linked to these words. The idea is that non-content words may take neighboring words as arguments, but dependencies are typically very local. The genuine keywords, ranked 100–1000, may be heads of dependents further away, and we therefore add edges between these words w_i and their neighboring words w_j if $|i - j| \leq 4$.

Head-initial/head-final. It is standard in unsupervised dependency parsing to compare against a structural baseline; either left-attach, i.e. all words attach to their left neighbor, or right-attach. Which structural baseline is used depends on the language in question. It is thus assumed that we know enough about the language to know what structural baseline performs best. It is therefore safe to incorporate this knowledge in our unsupervised parsers; our parsers are still as "unsupervised" as our baselines. If a language has a strong left-attach baseline, like Bulgarian, the first word in the sentence is likely to be very central for reasons of economy of processing. The language is likely to be head-initial. On the other hand, if a language has a strong right-attach baseline, like Turkish, the last word is likely to be central. The language is likely to be head-final. Some languages like Slovene have strong ($< 20\%$) left-attach *and* right-attach baselines, however. We incorporate the knowledge that a language has a strong left-attach or right-attach baseline if more than one third of the dependencies are attachments to a immediate left, resp. right, neighbor. Specifically, we add edges from all nodes to the first element in the sentence if a language has a strong left-attach baseline; and from all edges to the last (non-punctuation) element in the sentence if a language has a strong right-attach baseline.

Word inequality. An edge is added between two words if they have different word forms. It is not very likely that a dependent and a head have the same word form.

Cluster equality. An edge is added between two words if they are neighbors or neighbors' neighbors and belong to the same clusters. If so, the two words may be conjoined.

Morphological inequality. If two words w_i, w_j in the same context ($|i - j| \leq 4$) share prefix or suffix, i.e. the first or last three letters, we add an edge between them.

2.2 Edges using POS

Verb edges. All words are attached to all words with a POS tag beginning with "V...".

Finally, when we have access to POS information, we do not rely on vine edges besides left-attach, and we do not rely on keyword edges or suffix edges either.

[3]The search was simplified considerably. For example, we only considered symmetric context windows, where left context length equals length of right context, and we binned this length considering only values 1, 2, 4, 8 and all.

2.3 Ranking

Given the constructed graph we rank the nodes using the algorithm in Page and Brin (1998), also known as PageRank. The input to this algorithm is any directed graph $G = \langle E, V \rangle$ and the output is an assignment $PR : V \rightarrow \mathbb{R}$ of a score, also referred to as PageRank, to each vertex in the graph such that all scores sum to 1. A simplified version of PageRank can be defined recursively as:

$$PR(v) = \Sigma_{w \in B_v} \frac{PR(w)}{L(w)}$$

where B_v is the set of vertices such that $(w, v) \in E$, and $L(w)$ is the number of outgoing links from w, i.e. $|\{(u, u')|(u, u') \in E, u = w\}|$. In addition to this, Page and Brin (1998) introduces a so-called damping factor to reflect that fact that Internet users do not continue crawling web sites forever, but restart, returning to random web sites. This influences centrality judgments and therefore should be reflected in the probability assignment. Since there is no obvious analogue of this in our case, we simplify the PageRank algorithm and do not incorporate damping (or equivalent, set the damping factor to 1.0).

Note, by the way, that although our graphs are non-weighted and directed, like a graph of web pages and hyperlinks (and unlike the text graphs in Mihalcea and Tarau (2004), for example), several pairs of nodes may be connected by multiple edges, making a transition between them more probable. Multiple edges provide a coarse weighting of the underlying minimal graph.

2.4 Example

In Figure 1, we see an example graph of word nodes, represented as a matrix, and a derived dependency structure.[4] We see that there are four edges from *The* to *market* and six from *The* to *crumbles*, for example. We then compute the PageRank of each node using the algorithm described in Page and Brin (1998); see also Figure 1. The PageRank values rank the nodes or the words. In Sect. 3, we describe a method for building a dependency tree from

from/to	The	market	crumbled	.
The	0	4	6	3
market	4	0	5	3
crumbled	4	4	0	4
.	3	4	6	0
PR(%)	22.8	24.1	30.3	22.7

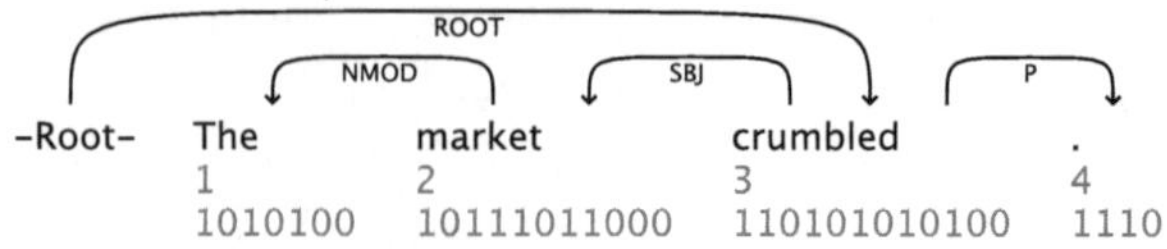

Figure 1: Graph, pagerank (PR) and predicted dependency structure for sentence 5, PTB-III Sect. 23.

a ranking of the nodes. This method will produce the correct analysis of this sentence; see Figure 1. This is because the PageRank scores reflect syntactic superiority; the root of the sentence typically has the highest rank, and the least important nodes are ranked lowly.

3 From ranking of nodes to dependency trees

Consider the example in Figure 1 again. Once we have ranked the nodes in our dependency structure, we build a dependency structure from it using the parsing algorithm in Figure 2. The input of the graph is a list of ranked words $\pi = \langle n_1, \ldots, n_m \rangle$, where each node n_i corresponds to a sentence position $n_{pr2ind(i)}$ decorated by a word form $w_{pr2ind(i)}$, where $pr2ind : \{1, \ldots, m\} \rightarrow \{1, \ldots, m\}$ is a mapping from rank to sentence position.

The interesting step in the algorithm is the head selection step. Each word is assigned a head taken from all the previously used heads and the word to which a head was just assigned. Of these words, we simply select the closest head. If two possible heads are equally close, we select the one with highest PageRank.

Our parsing algorithm runs in $\mathcal{O}(n \log n)$, since it runs over the ranked words in a single pass considering only previously stored words as possible heads, and guarantees connectivity, acyclicity and single-headedness, and thus produces well-formed non-projective dependency trees. To see this, remember that wellformed dependency trees are such that all nodes but the artificial root nodes have a single incoming edge. This follows immediately from

[4]The dependency structure in Figure 1 contains dependency labels such as 'SBJ' and 'ROOT'. These are just included for readability. We follow the literature on unsupervised dependency parsing and focus only on unlabeled dependency parsing.

1: $\pi = \langle n_1, \ldots, n_m \rangle$ # the ranking of nodes
2: $H = \langle n_0 \rangle$ # possible heads
3: $D = \emptyset$ # dependency structure
4: $pr2ind : \{1, \ldots, m\} \rightarrow \{1, \ldots, m\}$ # a mapping from rank to sentence position
5: **for** $n_i \in \pi$ **do**
6:   **if** $|H|$=1 **then**
7:     $c = 0$ # used to ensure single-headedness
8:   **else**
9:     $c = 1$
10:   **end if**
11:   $n_{j'} = \arg\min_{n_j \in H[c:]} |pr2ind(i) - pr2ind(j)|$ # select head of w_j
12:   $H = n_i \cup H$ # make n_i a possible head
13:   $D = \{(w_{pr2ind(i)} \leftarrow w_{pr2ind(j')})\} \cup D$ # add new edge to D
14: **end for**
15: **return** D

Figure 2: Parsing algorithm.

the fact that each node is assigned a head (line 11). Furthermore, the dependency tree must be acyclic. This follows immediately from the fact that a word can only attach to a word with higher rank than itself. Connectivity follows from the fact that there is an artificial root node and that all words attach to this node or to nodes dominated by the root node. Finally, we ensure single-headedness by explicitly disregarding the root node once we have attached the node with highest rank to it (line 6–7). Our parsing algorithm does not guarantee projectivity, since the iterative graph-based ranking of nodes can permute the nodes in any order.

4 Experiments

We use exactly the same experimental set-up as Gillenwater et al. (2010). The edge model was developed on development data from the English Penn-III treebank (Marcus et al., 1993), and we evaluate on Sect. 23 of the English treebanks and the test sections of the remaining 11 treebanks, which were all used in the CoNLL-X Shared Task (Buchholz and Marsi, 2006). Gillenwater et al. (2010) for some reason did not evaluate on the Arabic and Chinese treebanks also used in the shared task. We also follow Gillenwater et al. (2010) in only evaluating our parser on sentences of at most 10 non-punctuation words and in reporting unlabeled attachment scores excluding punctuation.

4.1 Strictly unsupervised dependency parsing

We first evaluate the strictly unsupervised parsing model that has no access to POS information. Since we are not aware of other work in strictly unsupervised multi-lingual dependency parsing, so we compare against the best structural baseline (left-attach or right-attach) and the standard DMV-EM model of Klein and Manning (2004). The latter, however, *has* access to POS information and should not be thought of as a baseline. Results are presented in Figure 3.

It is interesting that we actually outperform DMV-EM on some languages. On average our scores are significantly better ($p < 0.01$) than the best structural baselines (3.8%), but DMV-EM with POS tags is still 3.0% better than our strictly unsupervised model. For English, our system performs a lot worse than Seginer (2007).

4.2 Unsupervised dependency parsing (standard)

We then evaluate our unsupervised dependency parser in the more standard scenario of parsing sentences annotated with POS. We now compare ourselves to two state-of-the-art models, namely DMV PR-AS 140 and E-DMV PR-AS 140 (Gillenwater et al., 2010). Finally, we also report results of the IBM model 3 proposed by Brody (2010) for unsupervised dependency parsing, since this is the only recent pro-

	baseline	EM	ours
Bulgarian	37.7	37.8	**41.9**
Czech	**32.5**	29.6	28.7
Danish	43.7	**47.2**	43.7
Dutch	**38.7**	37.1	33.1
English	33.9	**45.8**	36.1
German	27.2	35.7	**36.9**
Japanese	44.7	52.8	**56.5**
Portuguese	35.5	**35.7**	35.2
Slovene	25.5	**42.3**	30.0
Spanish	27.0	**45.8**	38.4
Swedish	30.6	**39.4**	34.5
Turkish	36.6	**46.8**	45.9
AV	34.5	41.3	38.3

Figure 3: Unlabeled attachment scores (in %) on raw text. (EM baseline has access to POS.)

posal we are aware of that departs significantly from the DMV model. The results are presented in Figure 4.

Our results are on average significantly better than DMV PR-AS 140 (2.5%), and better than DMV PR-AS 140 on 8/12 languages. E-DMV PR-AS 140 is slightly better than our model on average (1.3%), but we still obtain better results on 6/12 languages. Our results are a lot better than IBM-M3. Naseem et al. (2010) report better results than ours on Portuguese, Slovene, Spanish and Swedish, but worse on Danish.

5 Error analysis

In our error analysis, we focus on the results for German and Turkish. We first compare the results of the strictly unsupervised model on German with the results on German text annotated with POS. The main difference between the two models is that more links to verbs are added to the sentence graph prior to ranking nodes when parsing text annotated with POS. For this reason, the latter model improves considerably in attaching verbs compared to the strictly unsupervised model:

acc	strict-unsup	unsup
NN	43%	48%
NE	41%	39%
VVFIN	31%	100%
VAFIN	9%	86%
VVPP	13%	53%

While the strictly unsupervised model is about as good at attaching nouns as the model with POS, it is much worse attaching verbs. Since more links to verbs are added, verbs receive higher rank, and this improves f-scores for attachments to the artificial root node:

f-score	strict-unsup	unsup
to_root	39.5%	74.0%
1	62.3%	69.6%
2	7.4%	24.4%
3–6	0	22.4%
7	0	0

This is also what helps the model with POS when parsing the example sentence in Figure 5. The POS-informed parser also predicts longer dependencies.

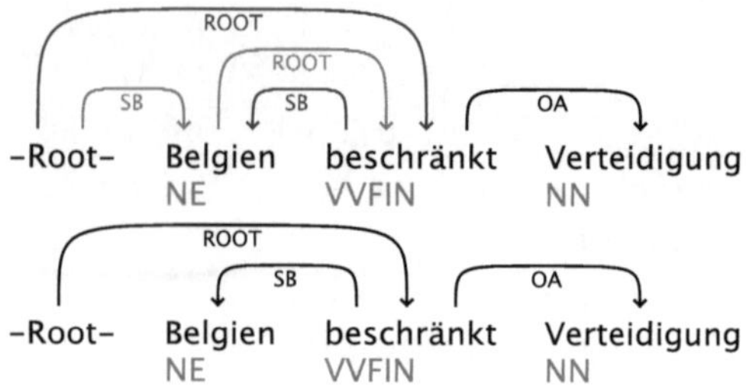

Figure 5: Predicted dependency structures for sentence 4 in the German test section; strictly unsupervised (above) and standard (below) approach. Red arcs show wrong decisions.

The same pattern is observed in the Turkish data, but perhaps less dramatically so:

acc	strict-unsup	unsup
Noun	43%	42%
Verb	41%	51%

The increase in accuracy is again higher with verbs than with nouns, but the error reduction was higher for German.

f-score	strict-unsup	unsup
to_root	57.4%	90.4%
1	65.7%	69.6%
2	32.1%	26.5%
3–6	11.6%	24.7%
7	0	12.5%

The parsers predict more long dependencies for Turkish than for German; precision is generally good, but recall is very low.

6 Conclusion

We have presented a new approach to unsupervised dependency parsing. The key idea is that a depen-

	DMV PR-AS 140	E-DMV PR-AS 140	ours	IBM-M3
Bulgarian	54.0	**59.8**	52.5	
Czech	32.0	**54.6**	42.8	
Danish	42.4	47.2	**55.2**	41.9
Dutch	37.9	46.6	**49.4**	35.3
English	61.9	**64.4**	50.2	39.3
German	39.6	35.7	**50.4**	
Japanese	**60.2**	59.4	58.3	
Portuguese	47.8	49.5	**52.8**	
Slovene	50.3	**51.2**	44.1	
Spanish	**62.4**	57.9	52.1	
Swedish	38.7	41.4	**45.5**	
Turkish	53.4	56.9	**57.9**	
AV	48.4	**52.2**	50.9	

Figure 4: Unlabeled attachment scores (in %) on text annotated with POS.

dency structure also expresses centrality or saliency, so by modeling centrality directly, we obtain information that we can use to build dependency structures. Our unsupervised dependency parser thus works in two stages; it first uses iterative graph-based ranking to rank words in terms of centrality and then constructs a dependency tree from the ranking. Our parser was shown to be competitive to state-of-the-art unsupervised dependency parsers.

References

Eneko Agirre and Aitor Soroa. 2009. Personalizing pagerank for word sense disambiguation. In *EACL*.

Samuel Brody. 2010. It depends on the translation: unsupervised dependency parsing via word alignment. In *EMNLP*.

Sabine Buchholz and Erwin Marsi. 2006. CoNLL-X shared task on multilingual dependency parsing. In *CoNLL*.

Shay Cohen, Kevin Gimpel, and Noah Smith. 2008. Unsupervised bayesian parameter estimation for dependency parsing. In *NIPS*.

Gregory Druck, Gideon Mann, and Andrew McCallum. 2009. Semi-supervised learning of dependency parsers using generalized expectation criteria. In *ACL-IJCNLP*.

Jason Eisner and Noah A. Smith. 2005. Parsing with soft and hard constraints on dependency length. In *IWPT*.

K Ganesan, C Zhai, and J Han. 2010. Opinosis: a graph-based approach to abstractive summarization of highly redudant opinions. In *COLING*.

Jennifer Gillenwater, Kuzman Ganchev, Joao Graca, Fernando Pereira, and Ben Taskar. 2010. Sparsity in dependency grammar induction. In *ACL*.

Dan Klein and Christopher Manning. 2004. Corpus-based induction of syntactic structure: models of dependency and constituency. In *ACL*.

Mitchell Marcus, Mary Marcinkiewicz, and Beatrice Santorini. 1993. Building a large annotated corpus of English: the Penn Treebank. *Computational Linguistics*, 19(2):313–330.

Ryan McDonald, Fernando Pereira, Kiril Ribarov, and Jan Hajič. 2005. Non-projective dependency parsing using spanning tree algorithms. In *HLT-EMNLP*.

Rada Mihalcea and Paul Tarau. 2004. Textrank: bringing order into texts. In *EMNLP*.

Tahira Naseem, Harr Chen, Regina Barzilay, and Mark Johnson. 2010. Using universal linguistic knowledge to guide grammar induction. In *EMNLP*.

Joakim Nivre. 2009. Non-projective dependency parsing in expected linear time. In *ACL-IJCNLP*.

Larry Page and Sergey Brin. 1998. The anatomy of a large-scale hypertextual web search engine. In *International Web Conference*.

Yoav Seginer. 2007. Fast unsupervised incremental parsing. In *ACL*.

Noah Smith and Jason Eisner. 2005. Contrastive estimation: training log-linear models on unlabeled data. In *ACL*.

Noah Smith and Jason Eisner. 2006. Annealing structural bias in multilingual weighted grammar induction. In *COLING-ACL*.

David Smith and Jason Eisner. 2009. Parser adaptation and projection with quasi-synchronous grammar features. In *EMNLP*.

Valentin Spitkovsky, Hiyan Alshawi, and Daniel Jurafsky. 2009. Baby steps: how "less is more" in unsupervised dependency parsing. In *NIPS Workshop on Grammar Induction, Representation of Language and Language Learning*.

Valentin Spitkovsky, Hiyan Alshawi, Daniel Jurafsky, and Christopher Manning. 2010. Viterbi training improves unsupervised dependency parsing. In *CoNNL*.

Kathrin Spreyer, Lilja Øvrelid, and Jonas Kuhn. 2010. Training parsers on partial trees: a cross-language comparison. In *LREC*.

Author Index

Association for Computational Linguistics
209 N. Eighth Street
Stroudsburg, Pennsylvania 18360

CURRAN ASSOCIATES INC
proceedings.com